What Readers are Saying!

"This is the New Age **Color Me Beautiful**."

"I feel enlightened!"

"This really cleared up something for me!"

"Boy, you nailed me on the button!"

"I wouldn't have believed it, but it really works!"

"Nobody knows that part of me."

"I just couldn't resist the questionnaire."

"Great fun!"

POWER COLOR!

POWER COLOR!

HOW TO ATTRACT ROMANCE, WEALTH, YOUTH, VITALITY AND MORE

Julia M. Busch
with Hollye Davidson

Kosmic Kurrents

P.O. BOX 141489 • CORAL GABLES, FLORIDA 33114 • USA

The purpose of this book is to educate and entertain. Any application of the concepts and/or information contained in this book is done solely at the risk and the discretion of the reader.

Portrait of *Julia* (inside front cover) by Hollye Davidson.
Book and cover design by Julia M.Busch.

Kosmic Kurrents books are available at special discounts for bulk purchases for premiums, fund-raising, sales promotions or educational use. Special editions or book excerpts can be composed to specification. For details, contact:

Marketing Department
Kosmic Kurrents
P.O. Box 141489
Coral Gables, Florida 33114

Publisher's Cataloging in Publication
Busch, Julia M., 1940-
Power color! how to attract romance, wealth, youth , vitality and more / Julia M. Busch with Hollye Davidson.
p. cm.
Includes bibliographical references.
Preassigned LCCN: 94-075321.
ISBN 0-9632907-1-1
1. Beauty, Personal. 2. Color of man. 3. Cosmetics. 4. Color in clothing. I. Davidson, Hollye. II. Title.
RA 778.B87 1994 646.7
QB194-559

Kosmic Kurrents
is an imprint of ANTI-AGING PRESS, INC.
P.O. BOX 141489 • CORAL GABLES, FLORIDA 33114 • USA

To
The Power
in a
Prism!

ACKNOWLEDGMENTS

Although I have, in fact, written this book, it could never have become a reality without the unique and artistic talents of colorist and painter Hollye Davidson, a dear friend and former student. Over a good many years, we have, together, formulated the information given in this book. We tested and retested, questioned family, close friends, acquaintances and strangers, handing our *questionnaire* to anyone who was just "there" and had the few minutes to participate. A great time was had by all, and I thank each and every one who took part.

Special acknowledgments, also, to Lynn Whittick and Shirlee Dreyer for proof reading, Scherley Busch Photography, Miami, FL, Shirlee Dreyer and Wally Engelhard of Engelhard Printing, Miami, FL, and Joan Mangrum of Braun-Brumfield for invaluable advice and meticulous production assistance.

And, as always, "Mom" whose enthusiasm, caring, dinners and snacks keep us all going.

TABLE OF CONTENTS

ABOUT THE ORIGINATORS

Two multi-faceted personalities *who truly know that riches exist not only at the end of the rainbow, but shimmer through every radiant drop,* Julia Busch and Hollye Davidson couldn't conceive of life without the multi-hued magnetic magic of color. Hollye documents her extraordinary color sense on exciting high-keyed canvases, painting the intricate sweeps of gossamer she sees dancing in, through and around her subjects. Julia, former teacher of drawing and composition at the University of Miami, Florida, humanities at Miami Dade Community College, jewelry designer, art historian, and portraitist with an incisive "eye", who also taught painting for many years has scrupulously researched and observed the character of color as it relates to energy and personality. As artists, they have worked together for almost 20 years, at first "painting" their concepts with brushes and then with words.

Publisher of Anti-Aging Press, writer on longevity and former co-host of Talk America's "Youthfully Yours", Julia Busch produces self-help books and cassette programs. Among them are the internationally known **Facelift Naturally, Treat Your Face Like a Salad!, Positively Young!,** and **Youth and Skin Secrets Revealed.** Hollye Davidson is President and CEO of Omnitech Gencorp, a computer concern.

THIS BOOK'S FOR YOU!

Have you been ogling Mr. Magnetic Smile for the past six months, waiting for tall, dark and energetic to just once flash his pearly whites your way? Or has that serious, strapping, button-down, briefcase-in-hand, rush-to-the-office type been brushing past your mooning glances without even the first look?

Maybe, you're on the other side of nature's mating magnet, desk drawer overflowing with battered ball points and punctured pencils, mutilated monuments to gnawing frustration each time ***Miss Lovely Long-Legged Lithe*** passes without so much as a nod.

Well, suffer no more! This book's for you.

Been battling the bulge without a budge? Frazzled nerves, foraging the fridge for a fortnight? Well, take a deep breath and keep reading. This book's for you.

Thirty and thirsty for a taste of that youthful Floridian fountain? ***Forty... fifty, and frenetic?*** Relax, this book's for you!

Need a penny pinching partner to balance your flights into fantasy finance? Or a compassionate colleague to stroke and soothe the bumps of business batterings? This book's for you.

You can fulfill your dreams with color. The right tones will titillate a tycoon, or vibrate a casual friendship into a volatile Vesuvius. You can color your way into a "just for fun" relationship, a business alliance, or a serious loving commitment.... "paint" yourself thinner, younger, richer and happier through the secret signals in the colors you wear, vibrate, visualize, breathe and project.

Just take the Color Test, find your Color Personality, and you are on your way!

Trust me, this book's for you!

THE POWER AND MEANING OF COLOR

Egypt knew. Atlantis knew. The ad and marketing industries know. Your interior decorator and psychologist know. Even plants know. Color is power! *Color is electromagnetic light-power vibrating through space.*

Exerting vital energy, visible and invisible to the human eye, it influences the mental, emotional and physical behavior of every living organism. Each one of us is a walking, talking, whirring electromagnet of colored light, emitting and attracting, radiating and absorbing, gravitating to and being repelled by a world of hues and tones. Whether color blind or acutely color oriented, we are color ourselves. We affect the color around us. And, seen or unseen, we are, likewise, modified by the tones in our environment.

Color has so affected us, that we even have a ***language of color.*** We *see red,* have a *mood indigo,* feel *deep purple.* Sometimes we are *really blue,* or *green with envy.* And, everyone knows the meaning of *"red hot mamma".*

Our culture gives us *color concepts*-we marry in white and mourn in black, while other cultures marry in red or bright colors and grieve in white. Traditional romantics seek perfect maidens fair, or tall, dark, swarthy masculine symbols of protection.

Universally we understand *color symbols*-"yellow" warnings, "Red" STOP signs and Emergencies. We all go on "green", and go for the "gold", which is also the "green".

Colors *arouse emotions* and reactions. With in-depth testing based on personal color preferences, psychologists can quite accurately sketch personality profiles. And check out the supermarket, you'll see a whole lot of raucous reds and radiant yellows. We are magically drawn to foods packaged in these colors, associating them with health and vitality--red and yellow also make the boxes look larger than they really are.

Color can soothe or enrage, calm or agitate. Ask any interior designer whose irate client has torn into the office screaming that a certain color drove him or her crazy.

Color has been shown to *instigate biological changes* in plants and in people. Lettuce grown under red glass can grow four times as quickly as in sunlight. Retarded or slow-learning children learn faster in yellow-colored rooms. A particular shade of pink tranquillizes violent or aggressive individuals. Pink is also one of the colors that can help control or reverse the effects of age.

Color can create *a sense of well-being.* You might have a "lucky color", or a color in which you feel, "high", "beautiful" or "in control". There are colors that can calm, balance and control digestion and food craving--color can aid in weight loss.

From the protective coloring and patterning of animals in the African Grasslands to the magnetic magic in the flash of the firefly, color has also fascinated naturalists. **Not only do nature's patterns and *colors protect,* but they *intuitively "signal"*** others of the same species. Do you know that you, too, right now, are "hiding or signaling" through the colors you are wearing? For instance, ladies, a little touch of red near the face, a scarf or a necklace, is very attractive to a man.

Much time has been spent studying the effects of color. Millions have been paid in research, for the expertise of psychologists and the advertising industry to market goods--and, with great success!

So, we too can take advantage of Color Power. With color, we can camouflage and protect at will, deliberately attract success, money, love, youth, a lithe slim body, friendships, business allies and more.

With the Power of Color we can do all this-*with great success!*

THE COLORFUL YOU!

The 17 Basic Personalities

(see back inside cover for color)

YOU ARE COLOR!

Oh whirring electromagnet of colored light, *you are color itself,* deriving your personal magnetism from the Basic Energies of RED, YELLOW and/or BLUE. *A Mini-Universe all your own, you are a unique blend that radiates a special glow.*

Just as a painter creates a vast palette from the Primaries-Red, Yellow and Blue, your personal illumination shimmers with all shades and tones from the Reds, Yellows and Blues to Purples, Oranges, and Greens. Your dancing energy sparkles with Turquoise, Chartreuse, Magenta and more. You are a **RAINBOW OF ENERGY**--*a Painting of Infinite Light!*

You may be a Primary Personality who takes on the energy personality of one of the three primary colors. Or, you may be a vibrant or subtle Blend of two or all three. Depending on your Individual Energy, you may be a *hard-driving **Red**, an ever-youthful **Canteloupe**, a serene **Blue**, a dreamy **Lavender**, a dazzling **Yellow**, a staunch **Brown**, a mysterious **Indigo**, or one of the many color/energy blends.*

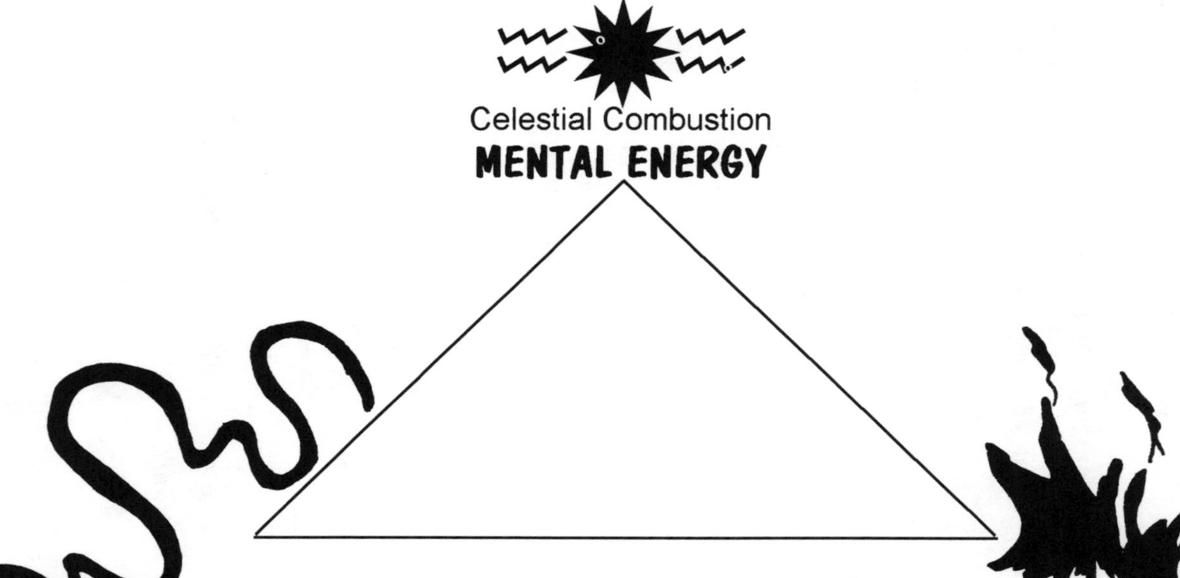

Basic Color-Energy Patterns

Basic Color-Energy Patterns

Long associated with *Mind, Body and Spirit,* the Three Basic Energies directly relate to the Three Primary Colors and each defines one of the Primary Personalities. Each Basic Energy has a distinctive basic rhythm and individual pattern.

***Equally powerful,* they differ in the manner in which their Force is Exerted. Yellow is traditionally linked with The Sun and Celestial Fire, Red with Earthly Fire and Physicality, and Blue with Air, Water and Spirituality.**

The energy of Red is one of vitality. Evenly directed, it is a one-way power, that travels like an arrow to its target. The rhythm continues straight ahead, never moving backward or sidewards. Personifying Fearless Arrogance, Red is an open, forceful, directed energy pattern that, in spite of all obstacles, goes directly to its destination. Like Earthly Fire, it is not an enduring one, tending to blaze, die down (sometimes from a loss of interest or exhaustion), and then, rekindle. Once rekindled, the consuming energy is aimed at the next target.

Very powerful in its fluid energy, Blue moves like the ancient meandering rivers. Its steady stream flows out in a quiet, sometimes plodding, rhythm. Personifying Subtle Persuasion, endurance is the key to the infinite strength of Blue.

The intense energy of Yellow charts a restless jagged pattern. Shooting out with great force, it overflows like the nuclear illumination of the Sun. Yellow traces a powerfully explosive, sporadic pattern. Searching and stumbling, evaluating and re-evaluating, weighing and measuring, Yellow personifies Rationalism and Reason.

From these Three Basic Energy patterns, all personality patterns develop. So, let's see where you fit in! You may be an intellectually oriented Yellow Personality who primarily uses your Mind, a Blue Individual who seeks the meaning of life through the Spirit, or a Red Persona who takes the bull by the physical horns and wrestles on a day-to-day here-and-now basis. Or you might be a Blend of Two or All Three of the Basic Energies. You could also be one of the Primary Personalities with Flashes of one or the other two. The combinations are many. Every individual is as different as the limitless colorful rainbow, but we can analyze ourselves through the Three Basic Patterns. Once we know who we are, we can see how we function, who and what we basically attract and adjust our "colors" accordingly to accomplish what we need.

CHARTING YOUR COLORSCOPE

We are each an *Ever-changing Rainbow, a Moving Light Projection that contains all the Colors of the Universe.* Every color imaginable is in every personality. Yet within all these colors, you can determine your underlying predominant color personality. The following questionnaire will lead you to its disclosure.

Take special care to ***answer the questions as they most apply to you.*** Except for definite male or female oriented questions, ***answer all the questions*** even if you feel the situation isn't applicable to your present circumstances. ***Answer as things really are,*** not as you think they should be, or the way you would like them to be. If you have difficulty in choosing one particular answer, eliminate the two that least apply. ***Answer as quickly as you can.***

Remember to answer all questions, and remember to answer as to the way you are.

Every Color is *Unique.* Each has its own *Magic and Excitement.*

The Questions

1. Are your love affairs *usually...*

A. Wild and passionate?

B. Stumbled into and out of with little or no commitment?

C. Enduring romances?

2. When going on a *blind date,* would you...

A. Prefer to go alone and meet for dinner?

B. Meet for lunch?

C. Go with another couple?

3. *Seeing the woman of your dreams,* would you...

A. Rush in, sweeping her off her feet, confident that you will overcome all obstacles?

B. Size her up, rationally balancing the workability of the situation, then ask her for a date?

C. Hope for, or arrange, an introduction by a third party?

4. Is *your ideal man...*

A. Someone to lean on, who will protect you, someone to cling to, and just generally be there?

B. Vital, aggressive and exciting... someone to keep up with?

C. Intelligent and rational, one who understands your need to be an individual?

5. When you *have to* tackle a difficult job, do you...

A. Jump in, work with great energy for a while, then get up, walk around, relax a little, knock out the kinks, maybe have a cup of coffee, get your second wind, then jump in again?

B. Work with a quiet easy rhythm until the job is completed?

C. Intensely work as quickly as possible using all the energy that you can muster, finish the job, then collapse?

6. *After a shopping spree,* are you likely to...

A. Return the purchase, because you bought it on a whim?

B. Hold on to the purchase, because it's yours and you'd feel badly if you didn't like it?

C. Give it to a friend if you really didn't need or want it, and not think another thought about it?

7. If a child runs to you with a minor injury, such as a skinned knee, would you...

A. Express sympathy, absolutely feeling the child's pain?

B. Advise the child to take note of the circumstances leading up to the incident and to learn from the experience?

C. Give the child a big hug and kiss, tell him it's going to be all right, and don't worry about it?

8. When "the romance is over", do you *generally*...

A. Review through tears, for months and months, all the wonderful times, clinging to the memories and all the "little things" that made the relationship so special?

B. Go on to the next affair and not look back?

C. Briefly review the situation, know that you were right and still feel a bit injured?

9. On a job interview, given the choice, would you *prefer to*...

A. Speak directly to the company president?

B. Be interviewed by the personnel director?

C. Meet first with your department head?

10. *Delayed at work,* your significant other phones home at the last minute. You have to adjust your plans to attend an *important function of a close friend and neighbor.* Would you...

A. Attend the party alone, because you have nothing better to do and had, after all, made the commitment?

B. Attend the party alone, because you know it will be fun and you'll have a great time?

C. Watch TV or keep busy around the house, while hoping your significant other will arrive in time to attend at least part of the festivities together?

11. You are *very involved* in a discussion you *feel very strongly* about. The discussion is about to get heated. Would you...

A. Know you are right and go down fighting?

B. Know you are right, but try to understand that there might be another side?

C. Know that you are right, but feel that the truth will come out in its own good time and not waste the energy on the fight?

12. As a suburban mother and at-home care provider *who has hired help*, would you...

A. Pick a job in the city, because it's higher paying and, after all, the reason you are working is to make the "extra ends" meet?

B. Take lower pay and work close to home just in case you have the chance to run home and cook for the family or tend to their other needs?

C. Take a good paying job with stature, confident that the hired help will manage things at home until you get there?

13. Evicted from his or her apartment unjustly, a friend turns to you. Would you...

A. Give your friend loving moral support and consolation, knowing just how he or she must "feel"?

B. "Feel" for your friend, but direct him or her to legal councel, because you feel a lawyer would be the best equipped to handle the job?
C. Want to go with your friend in order to help him or her confront the landlord with the truth of the situation?

14. If you, the man of the house and sole support of your family, had just been hired for a job with a *very good future,* but finances were going to be "tight" for a while and *your family was going to have to watch the "pennies" very closely in the meantime,* would you...

A. Look for and obtain a second high paying job, moonlight five days a week for a short time comfortably making ends meet until your regular position earns you more, confident that your energy will carry you through?
B. "Pinch" a while, because you feel your stature would be compromised by moonlighting, while knowing that the future will soon be brighter?
C. Get an extra job a couple of nights a week, preferably one that could be done at home, so that you can still be with the family while easing the burden?

Tabulating the Results

I'll bet you're wondering which color is best! Guess what? All of the colors are best. All are special. Each has a unique strength, talent and magic. Each hue has its dreams, romance and aspirations. Every color co-ordinates with its "color-mate" or "mates" in love and friendships and business endeavors--and all blend into the fascinating multi-hued tapestry of humanity.

Matching colors is fun, combining them is an art. So, artist, answers in hand, mentally ask yourself very quickly, "Have I answered the questions according to the way I react, not the way I would like to react, or think I should react?" Remember, this questionnaire is based on *energy patterns, and to correctly tabulate the results depends totally on your actual innate energy reactions.* You can aspire to react in a certain way, but that's another chapter. *Right now, we want to know what is!* We want to know where you fit into our Terrestrial Rainbow, so that you can begin to tune in to your Individual Color Personality, your Colorscope, your individual Color Vibrations.

The answers are coded. Each of the three symbols relates to a particular energy pattern. Check your answers against the following pages, omitting answers #3 and #14 if you are female, #4 and #12 if male.

The Answers

1. A– ◆
B– ●
C– ■

2. A– ◆
B– ●
C– ■

3. A– ◆(m)
B– ●
C– ■

4. A– ■(f)
B– ◆
C– ●

5. A– ●
B– ■
C– ◆

6. A– ●
B– ■
C– ◆

7. A– ■
B– ●
C– ◆

8. A– ■
B– ◆
C– ●

9. A– ◆
B– ●
C– ■

10. A– ●
B– ◆
C– ■

11. A– ◆
B– ●
C– ■

12. A– ◆(f)
B– ■
C– ●

13. A– ■
B– ●
C– ◆

14. A– ◆(m)
B– ●
C– ■

What's Your Score?

1. Count up your number of ■'s, ◆'s, & ●'s.

2. If all of your answers relate to *one symbol and one symbol only, go directly to the Configuration Sheet on the next page.*

3. If your answers relate to more than one symbol, and most of us will have a mixture, *arrange your configuration in descending order.* In other words, start with the symbol that appears most on your answer sheet. For instance, if you have, **7** ●'s, **3** ◆'s, and **2** ■'s, make sure the **7** ●'s (greatest number) starts first, and so on.

4. Match your individual configuration with the list on the Configuration Sheet.

Configuration Sheet

If you have the greatest number of ●'s, look here!

12●	Yellow
11●1■	Yellow
11●1◆	Yellow
10●2■	Yellow
10●2◆	Yellow
10●1■1◆	Yellow
10●1◆1■	Yellow
9●3■	Yellow with Chartreuse Flashes
9●3◆	Yellow with Canteloupe Flashes
9●2■1◆	Yellow with Chartreuse Flashes
9●2◆1■	Yellow with Canteloupe Flashes
8●4■	Chartreuse with Yellow Flashes
8●4■	Canteloupe with Yellow Flashes
8●3■1◆	Yellow with Chartreuse Flashes
8●3◆1■	Yellow/Canteloupe Blend
8●2■2◆	Chartreuse/Canteloupe Blend
8●2◆2■	Chartreuse/Canteloupe Blend
7●5■	Green with Orange Flashes
7●5◆	Orange with Canteloupe Flashes
7●4■1◆	Green with Yellow Flashes
7●4◆1■	Orange with Canteloupe Flashes
7●3■2◆	Chartreuse
7●3◆2■	Yellow with Canteloupe Flashes

6●6■	Green
6●6◆	Orange
6●5■1◆	Green with Magenta Flashes
6●5◆1■	Orange with Indigo Flashes
6●4■2◆	Olive with Canteloupe Flashes
6●4◆2■	Canteloupe
6●3■3◆	Olive/Canteloupe Blend
6●3◆3■	Olive/Canteloupe Blend
5●5■2◆	Green with Orange Flashes
5●5◆2■	Canteloupe with Chartreuse Flashes **or** Beige with Chartreuse Flashes
5●4■3◆	Green with Yellow Flashes
5●4◆3■	Brown with Chartreuse Flashes
4●4■4◆	Turquoise
4●4◆4■	Turquoise

If you have the greatest number of ◆'s, look here!

12◆	Red
11◆1●	Red
11◆1■	Red
10◆2●	Red
10◆2■	Red
10◆1●1■	Red
10◆1■1●	Red
9◆3●	Red with Salmon Flashes
9◆3■	Red with Magenta Flashes

9◆2●1■	Red with Salmon Flashes
9◆2●1■	Red with Magenta Flashes
8◆4●	Salmon with Red Flashes
8◆4■	Magenta with Red Flashes
8◆3●1■	Red/Salmon Blend
8◆3■1●	Red/Magenta Blend
8◆2●2■	Salmon/Magenta Blend
8◆2■2●	Magenta/Salmon Blend
7◆5●	Salmon
7◆5■	Purple with Magenta Flashes
7◆4●1■	Salmon
7◆4■1●	Magenta
7◆3●2■	Salmon with Blue Flashes
7◆3■2●	Plum with Magenta Flashes
6◆6●	Orange
6◆6■	Purple
6◆5●1■	Orange with Blue Flashes
6◆5■1●	Purple with Salmon Flashes
6◆4●2■	Salmon with Blue Flashes
6◆4■2●	Magenta with Salmon Flashes
6◆3●3■	Magenta/Plum Blend
6◆3■3●	Magenta/Plum Blend
5◆5●2■	Canteloupe with Chartreuse Flashes **or** Beige with Chartreuse Flashes
5◆5■2●	Plum with Salmon Flashes
5◆4●3■	Beige
5◆4■3●	Plum

4◆4●4■	Turquoise
4◆4■4●	Turquoise

If you have the greatest number of ■'s, look here!

12■	Blue
11■1●	Blue
11■1◆	Blue
10■2●	Blue
10■2◆	Blue
10■1●1◆	Blue
10■1◆1●	Blue
9■3●	Blue with Green Flashes
9■3◆	Blue with Indigo Flashes **or** Blue with Lavender Flashes
9■2●1◆	Blue with Green Flashes
9■2◆1●	Blue with Indigo Flashes **or** Blue with Lavender Flashes
8■4●	Blue/Green Blend
8■4◆	Indigo with Blue Flashes **or** Lavender with Blue Flashes
8■3●1◆	Blue/Green Blend
8■3◆1●	Blue/Indigo Blend **or** Blue/Lavender Blend

8■2●2◆	Blue/Indigo Blend **or** Blue/Lavender Blend
8■2◆2●	Blue/Indigo Blend **or** Blue/Lavender Blend
7■5●	Blue/Green Blend
7■5◆	Purple with Lavender Flashes
7■4●1◆	Green with Beige Flashes
7■4◆1●	Lavender with Purple Flashes
7■3●2■	Blue with Green Flashes
7■3◆2●	Indigo/Lavender Blend
6■6●	Green
6■6◆	Purple
6■5●1◆	Green with Lavender Flashes
6■5◆1●	Purple with Green Flashes
6■4●2◆	Blue/Green Blend
6■4◆2●	Indigo **or** Lavender
6■3●3◆	Brown
6■3◆3●	Brown
5■5●2◆	Green with Orange Flashes
5■5◆2●	Plum with Salmon Flashes
5■4●3◆	Olive
5■4◆3●	Indigo with Orange Flashes
4■4●4◆	Turquoise
4■4◆4●	Turquoise

YOUR COLORSCOPE: PERSONALITY PROFILES

So, my colorful friend, who are hue? What is your Personality Color... Your Unique Colorscope? Are you a "Primary" Red? Yellow? Blue? A "Secondary" Orange? Green? Purple? *(We are speaking strictly colorese. Believe me, these colors are second to none!)* Or, do you radiate another intriguing shade or tone? Perhaps, you are a "Blend"? You might even have "Flashes"! Could you be an "Either/Or"?

If you are a ***Straight* Color**, without blends or flashes, turn to the Personality Profiles to find your Colorscope.

Blends, you are a combination of *two* of the Basic Personality Colors. Through the mixture of both, you have created a totally new homogeneous Color Personality. If you have "scored" a Blend, read the two colors you have combined and see how you have borrowed from each. In some configurations there may be more of one color than the other, but, nevertheless, your personality is consistent and stable. Turn to the Personality Profiles and read the colors that merge to form your individual hue.

Do you have *Flashes?* First, it is important to know that we all have flashes of color from time to time, like the angry flash when we "see red", or become "green with envy"; these are fleeting color moods and reactions to life situations. A Basic Personality Flash is different. It is a particular color that flashes throughout your Basic Color Energy. It belongs to you and is not a temporary reaction to a circumstance. It is a strong and obvious energy change adding another fascinating dimension to your Colorscope. It can appear suddenly as an energy surge, an inspiration, or can act as a balancer. Compared to a Blend that is even-colored and consistent throughout, a Flash might be considered a momentary modifier that shoots through your Basic Energy Pattern. It is strong and it is obvious.

Two profiles having the same configuration, or "score", can have a *different rate of flashes* depending on heredity and environmental factors. And... an individual who *desires or aspires* to be the color of his or her Flashes, might "appear" to be the color of the Flashes. However, the underlying Basic Energy Color will remain consistent.

If you have Flashes in your configuration, to establish your total Colorscope, first, look up your Basic Color Personality, then check out your Flashes. *Also, see: The Aspiring You, for more information on Flashes.*

Are you an *Either/Or?* This happens very infrequently, and your Colorscope can very easily be determined by you.

Are you Indigo or Lavender? Both colors are blue-purples and both have the *same energy pattern. Indigo,* however, is a *very dense compact color that stays close to the Earth,* while *Lavender, having mixed with Air and Light, travels in dreamy realms.* So, exciting Blue/Purple, which are you?

Are you a Canteloupe or Beige? Both Canteloupe and Beige are colors of refinement--*refinement meaning an airy light-and-color mixture. Canteloupe is the refinement of vital and substantial Yellow/Orange.* It shares much in common with the energy and "ideals" of *Beige, which is the refinement of dense, earthy rich Brown.* Although they share the same "energy wave", their *approach or orientation differs.* Beige works with subdued inner strength and power, while Canteloupe is more overt in action. Read the two personalities and see which of the refined two is you!

RED

"I am powerful and emphatic about it!"

Configurations

12◆	
11◆1●	
11◆1■	
10◆2●	
10◆2■	
10◆1●1■	
10◆1■1●	
9◆3●	See Salmon for Flashes
9◆3■	See Magenta for Flashes
9◆2●1■	See Salmon for Flashes
9◆2●1■	See Magenta for Flashes
8◆3●1■	See Salmon for Blend
8◆3■1●	See Magenta for Blend

Red Personality Profile

Associated with Earthly Fire and Combustion, Red describes *Earth Energy and Physical Force.*

Along with Yellow and Blue, Red is one of the Three Primaries. It is from these three colors that all other colors are blended.

You saw it streak by, flashing, clanging, racing into battle. No mistake was made when the fire engine was painted red, or when the ancient gods were daubed a rosy hue to denote their supernatural powers. Dynamic and passionate, Red, you have all the intense power and excitement of the blaze, the fire-fighters and the streaking engine all performing at the same time. And you do love performing, being "on stage", vying, competing and winning with an energy that seems absolutely supernatural. You are positive directed energy. Powerful, you generously give your vital warmth to anyone who needs it.

You are physical, sensual, highly energetic--and you

know it! Beware of talking too much in the "I". Others might label you egocentric--not that you aren't, and not that there's anything wrong with self-love and respect, and not that your independent self would give a "hoot" anyhow--but to keep our terrestrial rainbow intact, it's best not to aver your self-homage too loudly, or too often. The other colors will think you a boor, or, otherwise, feel insecure around such tremendous enthusiasm.

You are, indeed, *a blaze.* If those fires sweep out of control, your generally impatient self can become exceedingly anxious. Over-stoking the fires can lead to a few restful days in bed. Cooling embers, however, will show your fickle side. One finds you quickly leaving situations out of sheer boredom and readily changing commitments without once looking back.

You are at your best, oh super one, with a purpose, enthusiastically challenging the whole color palette into action. For the sake of us all, we beg you to *stay at your best!*

YELLOW

"I am bright, warm, and I like to find the truth!"

Configurations

12●	
11●1■	
11●1◆	
10●2■	
10●2◆	
10●1■1◆	
10●1◆1■	
9●3■	See Chartreuse for Flashes
9●3◆	See Canteloupe for Flashes
9●2■1◆	See Chartreuse for Flashes
9●2◆1■	See Canteloupe for Flashes
8●3■1◆	See Chartreuse for Flashes
8●3◆1■	See Canteloupe for Blend
7●3◆2■	See Canteloupe for Blend

Yellow Personality Profile

Associated with the Sun and Stellar Combustion, Yellow describes *Celestial Energy and Mental Force!*

Along with Red and Blue, Yellow is one of the Three Primaries. It is from these three colors that all other colors are blended.

Well, hello Sunshine, and I mean Sunshine! You have the dazzle and brilliance of a bright summer day, or a sparkler on the Fourth of July. And like the Sun, your energy dances out in rays, shedding light on the truth wherever you find it. You are fast-paced, electric, strong and endure your own fast-pace well as you seek conceptual and intellectual understanding. You can be very open. Overflowing with warmth, attracting fun-loving, intellectual and ambitious friends, your lithe body is often seen in the midst of social gatherings, amiably chatting, searching for and shedding new light on most any subject.

When positive, you are the most rational of any color, but watch out for the flip side. In a negative frame of mind that lucid scientific mind of yours, that stumbles across many "truths", can run haywire, become prejudiced, dogmatic and irrational, turning the dancing rays of sunlight into a jagged clawing bolt of obstinacy. You then become unable to see anything but your own standpoint. Turn your electric energy against yourself and you self-destruct. Turn it against anyone else, and they had better head for the hills at the first sizzle of your current's discharge. The next one might be the beginning of an irrational storm no one deserves.

Often uncertain of your actions, the storm quickly subsides and clear shafts of light banish the raging torrents. Equally unaware of the impact of your actions, you can't understand the attitude of those who have had to weather your storm and may have fallen back to lick their wounds. Just remember that *positive thought is your key*, and you will warm the universe with your spectacular glow and charm, and clearly illuminate the way in your search for truth.

BLUE

(Ranges from Medium to Navy Blue)

Strong, I have truly found the Power in Passivity!"

Configurations

12■	10■2◆
11■1●	10■1●1◆
11■1◆	10■1◆1●
10■2●	
9■3●	See Green for Flashes
9■3◆	See Indigo and Lavender for Flashes
9■2●1◆	See Green for Flashes
9■2◆1●	See Indigo and Lavender for Flashes
8■4●	See Green for Blend
8■3●1◆	See Green for Blend
8■3◆1●	See Indigo and Lavender for Blend
8■2●2◆	See Indigo and Lavender for Blend
8■2◆2●	See Indigo and Lavender for Blend
7■5●	See Green for Blend
7■3●2■	See Green for Flashes
6■4●2◆	See Green for Blend

Blue Personality Profile

Associated with Ether and Water, the Fluid Upper Regions of Space and Deep Water, Blue *Describes Spiritual Force!*

Along with Red and Yellow, Blue is one of the Three Primaries. It is from these three that all other colors are blended.

Blue, you are one of the Powerful Primaries. Encompassing the serenity of the Upper Regions of Space and the Great Deep Waters below, *you have a special secret.* Like the proverbial "tortoise and the hare", your *knowledge of passive and powerful resistance* can quietly outdistance your hard-driving, fast-paced first cousins, Yellow and Red. Your energy streams constant and even-flowing.

Strong-willed and intense, you are mysteriously seductive. Coolly and sensually flowing out into the clear sky and crystalline waters, you spiritually refresh yourself and intuitively comfort those who need to drink from your revitalizing kindness. At your level best, you are fair. Carefully and sympathetically weighing all sides of a situation, you are constantly called upon by friends to exercise your acute judgement. At your talented best, you can display fresh and innovative artistic, poetic, musical or scientific expertise.

But, Blue, beware! Your are *very* sensitive. Easily shocked, you can disorient, your cool crystal waters slowing to dribbles that can submissively cling to the side of a sturdy rock or secure river bank. You might find yourself "stuck in the mud", dwelling on one subject, mulling it over and over. Or, if mental "skies" loom melancholy, you might take to the comfort of deep space and appear "flighty". You must take special care to stay mentally clear and physically active. Since you have the easiest road of all colors to develop your spiritual side, *you need to consciously balance both your mental and physicalness.* This accomplished, you can offer new knowledge through your great intuitive reservoir, serene sensual sensitivity and "wash" refreshing spiritual insight over our entire earthly color palette.

ORANGE

(Range includes Medium to Deep Orange and Tangerines)

"I am energetic, practical and I like to believe in a cause!"

Configurations

6◆6●
6●6◆
7●5◆ See Salmon for Flashes
7●4◆1■ See Canteloupe for Flashes
6●5■1◆ See Indigo for Flashes
6◆5●1■ See Blue for Flashes

Orange Personality Profile

Associated with Earthly Fire and Celestial Combustion, Orange describes *Physical and Mental force.*

Blending Primary Red and Yellow, Brilliant Orange is created. Along with Purple and Green, it is one of the Secondary Family of Colors.

Okay everybody, out of the way, Orange is taking center-stage. Enthusiastic, energetic and earthy, Orange, you are a performer *par excellence.* Versatile, you can do almost anything that deals with people, showmanship and prestige. Goal-oriented, you are a driving force, an ambitious leader and organizer. Practical, you like facts, striving for simplicity of thought. Athletic, you relate well physically. Hard working, you like your comforts. You are proud, happy and strive to be carefree.

Ah, but Orange, you are, also, a rationalizer par excellence, easily talking yourself in and out of commitments, preferring more surface than in-depth involvements. You like to rapidly skim the tide, flushing in the limelight, rather than explore the fruits of solemn profundities. Take care that you are not so on the move, or so busy taking ambitious bows that you become too proud, too materialistic, or too wrapped up in yourself that you deny credit that rightfully belongs to someone else.

Orange, you are the combination of Earth and Celestial Combustion. Blending Red and Yellow, you offer the hard-driving, fast-paced mental and physical energies of both. *Cultivate a little Blue in your aspirations; it will give you the spiritual balance you need.*

GREEN

(Range includes Medium to Forest to Kelly Greens)

"My strength is in my kindness!"

Configurations

6●6■	
6■6●	
8■4●	See Blue for Blend
8■3●1◆	See Blue for Blend
7■5●	See Blue for Blend
7●5■	See Yellow for Flashes
7■4●1◆	See Beige for Flashes
7●4■1◆	See Yellow for Flashes
6■5●1◆	See Lavender for Flashes
6●5■1◆	See Magenta for Flashes
6■4●2◆	See Blue for Blend
5■5●2◆	See Orange for Flashes
5●5■2◆	See Orange for Flashes
5●4■3◆	See Yellow for Flashes

Green Personality Profile

Associated with the Green Earth and Waters, Green describes a *Balance of Energies* as Earthly Tides and Growth Rhythms come into accord.

**Combining Primary Yellow and Blue,
Lush Green is created. Along with Orange and Purple,
Green is one of the Secondary Colors.**

Subtly strong, Green, you personify Strength in Kindness. Sensitive and feeling, you can be the most giving of all colors. Tuning yourself to the world around you, you blend Yellow Mental Energy and Blue Spiritual Travel, balancing the Earthly Forces and juggling the Tides and Growth Rhythms, as you seek harmony and serenity.

You are so "in tune" with your environment that you literally "move with the tides" around you, and a change in your surroundings can actually change you. At times, very methodical, you could search for a system of living, or a formula that will encompass "the meaning of it all". You actually are very good at understanding "things", easily blending the sciences and the arts.

Green, you are so kind, and so soft that you can be easily depressed. And, soooo giving! Take care that you don't become giving to a fault, and begin to feel cheated through the lack of others' appreciation. Also, watch that your search for serenity doesn't find you complacent, saturated, and jaded. The Earthly Tides may then wash a few extra barnacles around your belt line, and you'll begin formulizing a new "Battle of the Bulge".

Peace-loving, you don't always blend in with the crowd. You may enjoy a career with pets or flowers. Owning and running your own pet shop or floral boutique could be very satisfying. Family oriented, you can be an excellent preschool teacher, and your desire to "comprehend" could be fulfilled as an avid student of the social sciences. Your methodological mind sometimes seeks success in accounting, electronics, and the computer sciences, and quite possibly, the musical arts.

Green, you follow an ideal. Verdant and velvety, you tread lightly. You seek to get along with everyone, harmoniously offering a wealth of kindness in exchange for serenity.

PURPLE

(Range includes Royal Purples and Violets)

"I am strong, creative and have definite opinions."

Configurations

6■6◆	
6◆6■	
7◆5■	See Magenta for Flashes
7■5◆	See Lavender for Flashes
6◆5■1●	See Salmon for Flashes
6■5◆1●	See Green for Flashes

Purple Personality Profile

Associated with Earth Energy
Reflected through the Air,
Purple describes *Physical and Spiritual Force.*

Combining Primary Red and Blue,
Regal Purple is one of the Secondary Colors.

Powerful, dynamic and regal. Royal heritage has bestowed majestic power on you, the color of kings. And, like your imposing forbearers, you love P-O-W-E-R in order to be in control of your dominion and those who reside within it. High on a hill, you oversee your territory and rule your realm with a creative and *avant* mind. A free thinker, far from the crowd, you are fascinating to all who meet you. Intelligent, strong-willed and artistic, you, indeed, have all it takes to bear the royal banner. It's no wonder that you feel you are better than others.

Strong-willed, you are ever sensitive. Like a tuning fork, you vibrate to the emotions of others, keenly monitoring those around you. One foot in your physical realm, you reach out with your keen intuition into the spiritual and esoteric regions where you can easily lose yourself. Don't go too far afield, or stand so high on that hill that you lose touch with life and become fussy, neurotic, opinionated or melancholy. A royal life can be a lonely one. Or, it can be solid and fulfilling. Remember, even though your blood is Blue, you are Purple and "Purple" is one-half Red!

Stay and rule benevolently. Don't isolate.

CANTELOUPE

(Range includes Melon, Peach and Apricot)

"I am very artistic and lucid.
I have a graceful, youthful beauty
and I attract money!"

Configurations

6●4◆2■	
8●4◆	See Yellow for Flashes
8●3◆1■	See Yellow for Blend
8●2■2◆	See Chartreuse for Blend
8●2◆2■	See Chartreuse for Blend
6●3■3◆	See Olive for Blend
5●5◆2■	See Chartreuse for Flashes
5◆5●2■	See Chartreuse for Flashes

Canteloupe Personality Profile

Associated with Earth and Celestial Combustion, Canteloupe describes *Refined and Subdued Physical and Mental Force.*

Primary Yellow and Primary Red mix to create Secondary Orange. Extra Yellow is added to Orange and a Yellow-Orange Blend results. Air and Light refines the Yellow-Orange Blend until pastel Canteloupe emerges.

Dear charming, youthful Canteloupe, you are the envy of all those who seek the magical fountain. Exuding fluid softness, you enjoy admiration for your special beauty. You feel yourself untouchable, and in a way, you are. The years don't seem to weigh on your physicalness as they might on another color. Perhaps, it's your fascination with romantic ideals or an unconscious acceptance of "Tinkerbelle and Peter Pan" that keeps you young. If, indeed a fairy tale came true before your very eyes, you wouldn't be at all surprised. But, then again, maybe it's your striving to be gentle and generous that keeps you dewy fresh. Whatever the magic, you possess a quiet strength, energy and youthfulness through most of your years.

Very social and very lucid, you work well with people. But, take care that you don't become a "butter-fly", too lucid and too free, or you will confuse yourself and lose sight of your priorities.

Your *need for personal freedom* steers you clear of oppressive crowds where you feel choked, and right into your *love for money.* Sometimes stemming from a fear and insecurity of the future and sometimes, from a deep desire to be generous and philanthropic, money means personal freedom to you--and personal freedom is the one thing you value greatly.

Often very artistic, golden and glowing, don't con-fuse yourself with trivia. *Follow your heart, instinct and love of beauty.* You can be a special light.

BEIGE

(Range also includes Bone)

"I am sophisticated, conservative and strive for refinement!"

Configurations

5◆4●3■

5◆5●2■ See Chartreuse for Flashes

5●5◆2■ See Chartreuse for Flashes

Beige Personality Profile

Associated with Fixed Stable Energy, Beige describes *Sophistication and Tradition.*

Blending the Primaries-Red, Yellow and Blue, a rich Brown is created. Infusing the blend with Air and Light, Brown is refined to a Soft, Neutral Beige.

Beige, you are Refinement and Cultivation personified. Deeply rooted in the stable richness and substantiality of Brown, you nurture yourself through the Earth. Striving to branch out into intellectual and creative sophistication, you are the Refinement of Fixed Energy. Subdued and conservative, you have a deep appreciation for the arts and a healthy respect for wealth which you can, by the way, readily attract. You *like* yourself, exude confidence and, generally, have a feeling of well-being. Your balanced refined poise draws bright cultured people to your side, attracting those who desire to make a solid physical stand, and those who are hopeful of future assets.

You like to work and prefer not to be singled out, respectfully blending in with your own environment. Functioning particularly well in the business world, documentary film industry and advertising, you could easily be a writer or the "head" of a large concern. Neutral, but strong in purpose, you are usually the man or the woman "behind the scenes" quietly directing the action with a powerful hand and firm foothold.

Take care, Beige. Don't follow the "rules" too closely, or become too fastidious in your cultivation. You may become too strategic, too philosophical, overly dry, lack spontaneity or engender ennui. Also, take care not to elevate your elegance to such high-bred purity as to pale your delicate Beige into oblivion. Remember, always, your roots are in the rich deep Browns. As you reach out into the rarefied intellectual and cultural climes, continue to draw sustenance from your colorful earthly heritage.

CHARTREUSE

(Range includes some shades of Lime)

"I am electric, exciting, avant garde and to the point!"

Configurations

7●3■2◆	
8●4■	See Yellow for Flashes
8●2■2◆	See Canteloupe for Blend
8●2◆2■	See Canteloupe for Blend

Chartreuse Personality Profile

Yellow Celestial Combustion infuses with Green Balance of Forces to short-circuit Earthly Balance causing Change. Chartreuse is associated with *Modernization!*

Primary Yellow and Primary Blue mix to create Secondary Green. Extra Yellow is added to Green and Chartreuse emerges!

Fresh as a spring garden after an April rain, Chartreuse, you combine Yellow and Green. Blending Celestial Combustion with the Fluid Regions of Upper Space and the Earthly Tides and Growth Rhythms, you instigate the *avant garde* in thought. Short-circuiting the earthly humdrum, you cause physical change to occur. You are modern, bright, and electric. Highly inventive, you like crisp new ideas. Full of life, you'll try anything, going wherever your active libido carries you. One might find you sky-diving or racing cars. Whatever the activity, you'll try it--at least once! You are so totally open to new thought and the *business of living.*

With all your mental, spiritual and physical whirl-winds, you are really very introverted in your personal life, tending to avoid highly intimate relationships. It's not that you are not curious or caring about people, it's just that you cannot handle stress well. Heavy relationships tend to bog you down. Pressures confuse you and can make you angry and volatile. *Your basic need for clarity and freshness* must be met or you become hyper in the extreme. It's merely your nature, *oh inventor and instigator of change.* Like the dazzling green grasshopper in the dewy verdance, and the electric flash of a butterfly in the sunlight, you bring newness and excitement, brightness and the avant garde to an otherwise plodding planet!

TURQUOISE

(Range includes Aqua)

"I am solid, but flexible and I love change!"

Configurations

4●4■4◆

4●4◆4■

4◆4●4■

4◆4■4●

4■4◆4◆

4■4●4●

Turquoise Personality Profile

As Blue Spiritual Force infuses with Green Earthly Balance, Turquoise *Spiritual and Physical Change* is born.

Primary Yellow mixes with Primary Blue to create Secondary Green. Extra Blue is added to Green and Turquoise emerges.

Now you see it! Now you don't! Watch carefully friends! A veritable chameleon of quick changes, will the real Turquoise please stand up? Spontaneous, fun and exciting, Turquoise, you love transition, but this doesn't mean that you don't make commitments. In fact, although quite independent, you are *solid.* Flexible, you are definitely *purposeful.* There are explicit reasons for each and every change you make. A gracious *seeker of knowledge,* you are hopeful, open, and accepting of new ideas and situations, attracting other "explorers" and "searchers" along the way.

Next to Magenta, you are the most spontaneous in our rainbow of personalities. But, take care to remember why you are making your "alterations". Keep in mind the purpose behind each image, or you can lose yourself in your own "projection". Instead of the rabbit, you might just find yourself being the hat. And like a vaporous hologram, you, all-of-a-sudden, are surprised to find that you aren't what you thought you were.

A genuine three-ring-circus, you must remember to focus on the needs of others. While "keeping up appearances", keep everything in its place or you can get too wrapped up in your own "show".

Albeit, one thing is certain, you are great fun and exciting to be with. *Surprise is the name and change is the game!*

LAVENDER

(Range includes Lilac-Purples)

"I am romantic and enjoy warm, soft, gentle surroundings!"

Configurations

6■4◆2●

8■4◆ — See Blue for Flashes

8■3◆1● — See Blue for Blend

8■2◆2● — See Blue for Blend

8■2●2◆ — See Blue for Blend

7■4◆1● — See Purple for Flashes

7■3◆2● — See Indigo for Blend

Lavender Personality Profile

Associated with Earth Energy Reflected into Air and the Upper Regions of Space, Lavender describes *Refined and Subdued Spiritual Force.*

Primary Blue mixes with Primary Red to create Secondary Purple. Blue is again added to Purple resulting in a Blue-Purple Blend. Infusing the Blend with Air and Light, the Blue-Purple is refined to a pastel, delicate Lavender.

Ah, Lavender--------dreamy, dreamy Lavender. You live in pale puffs of tinted gossamer, ever-hopeful of eternal optimism and continually seeking the *illusive* "happy ending". The ultimate romantic, you can see yourself as the perfect Guinevere or conquering Gallahad, shining, stately and serene. You love beauty and deeply appreciate subtle nuance. Drawing quiet sympathy from the pale Blue tints in your soft Lavender, you *strive* to be thoughtful to those around you. Sentimental in the extreme, and ever "wary" of in-depth feelings, you shy away from intensely passionate relationships for fear that the highly emotional you will plunge from the clouds into the void of despair. Deep down you know you can be very pessimistic and easily overtaken by sadness. Ever on guard, the first signs of trouble find you quietly and *quickly* ascending to your spiritual shelf.

When you are positive in thought, you can be *very* strong-minded, convincingly weaving romantic dreams that, many times, come true. But take care! You can all too easily change your mind when uncertain.

Truly traditional, your *self* pulls against your *yearnings* to be a free spirit and you become insecure. Take care to keep your dreams practical and you can constructively plant your castles on the Earth, making romance a reality for yourself and for those you love,

INDIGO

(Range Includes deep, deep Blue-Purples)

"I am intense and intuitive. Feeling deeply for mankind, I know that I am an integral part of the entire Universe!"

Configurations

6■4◆2●	
8■4◆	See Blue for Flashes
8■3◆1●	See Blue for Blend
8■2◆2●	See Blue for Blend
8■2●2◆	See Blue for Blend
7■4◆1●	See Purple for Flashes
7■3◆2●	See Indigo for Blend

Indigo Personality Profile

Associated with Earth Energy Reflected into Air and Water, Indigo describes *Intuition and Mystery!*

Primary Blue blends with Primary Red to create Secondary Purple. Deep Blue is, again, added to Purple, and deep Indigo emerges!

Deep, deep pools of inky mystery, Indigo, you are a keeper of many secrets. Powerful, you make no blatant show of strength. Many are fooled by your easy-going "appearance", but you definitely do not move with the tide. Your innate wisdom finds you, many times, cast in the role of sagacious confidant and friend. Trustworthy, an oath sworn by an Indigo, is an oath sworn forever.

You have a psychic fascination with the past. Intuitive, your quiet determination is mystically drawn to ancient civilizations. Nothing half-way about you. You delve deeply into your subjects making you an excellent writer, and very possibly, an archeologist.

With a strong love of beauty and the Universe, you are interested in many things, past, present and future. Generally non-conformist in nature, however, your religious interpretations of the Laws of the Universe take on intense individuality. Very, very serious, and easily bored, you need to "lighten up" a little and cultivate your sense of humor (if you haven't already). Usually a loner, Indigo, you really do enjoy people. Once you learn to laugh, you can be wonderful fun!

SALMON

(Range includes Tomato and Coral)

"I am proud, energetic and communicative.
I will astound you!"

Configurations

7◆5●	
7◆4◆1■	
8◆4●	
8◆3◆1■	See Red for Flashes
8◆2■2●	See Red for Blend
8◆2◆2■	See Magenta for Blend
7◆3●2■	See Magenta for Blend
6◆4●2■	See Blue for Flashes

Salmon Personality Profile

Associated with Earth Combustion, Salmon describes *Refined and Subdued Physical Force.*

Primary Red and Primary Yellow mix to create Secondary Orange. Extra Red is added to Orange and a Red-Orange Blend results. Air and Light combine to refine the Red-Orange to a delicate vibrant Salmon.

There you go astounding people again! The sensuous silver-tongued orator, Salmon, you weave a silken spell around what appears to be a totally captivated audience. Bright and alert, you seem to all "bigger than life", ever-questioning and showing off your personal knowledge.

Hard-working, energetic and curious, like your aquatic namesake, you swim upstream well--your silver tongue dazzling those around you.

You can be possessive and demanding. Your questions can be a bit condescending. And, you can definitely rub a few people the wrong way. But so many don't mind.

So many are seductively amazed, or amazingly seduced, by all the little tidbits of information that you garner that they don't even see that streak of snobbish bossiness that surfaces every now and then.

Although a leader, you are seldom in the *avant garde,* taking on the more physical and earthy aspects of your Red cousin. You prefer to be the boss, but your hard-driving enthusiasm finds you also working for, and with, others.

You are competitive, yet sensitive, forward looking, challenging without being overbearing--you enjoy life and humanity!

OLIVE

(Range includes Khaki, Pea Green, Avocado and Moss Green)

"I am secure, practical and interested in the Unusual!"

Configurations

5■4●3◆

6●4■2◆ See Canteloupe for Flashes

6●3■3◆ See Canteloupe for Blend

6●3◆3■ See Canteloupe for Blend

Olive Personality Profile

Associated with the Fixed Stable Energy of Brown pulling toward Green Earth Growth Rhythms, Olive describes *Stable Balance.*

Blending the Primaries Yellow and Blue, Green is created. A little extra Yellow, some Red and a drop of Blue mix to establish a Velvety Olive.

Olive, you balance Earthly Tides and Growth Rhythms with Fixed Stable Earth richness, creating a lush Green-Brown. Solid and enduring, warm and sympathetic, it's no wonder the olive branch has been designated the symbol of peace. Traditional and practical, you do, indeed, *cherish tranquility.* Keeping your life on an even keel, you invest in life insurance and other buffers, safeguarding yourself against possible upheavals. Hard working, you are *very realistic.* Ever-hopeful, you don't hold idle dreams, preferring to move with the pragmatic norm.

Drawn, however, to the exotic, you enjoy science fiction and "scary" movies, have the most interesting friends and would be very comfortable on safari or on an archeological dig.

With *deep respect* for, and strong interest in, uncovering the mysteries of nature, you, sometimes, gravitate to the sciences for a career. One can readily find you in the fields of geology, biology and botany. Open minded to others, you make a good personnel director or salesperson. Patient and sympathetic, you can be an excellent teacher or trainer. *Accepting without modifying* yourself, you are an excellent reporter who seeks to understand the human predicament.

Oh, omni-tranquil Olive, take care that your desire for peace doesn't find you too entrenched, too subdued, plodding or "set" in your ways. Watch that the "pendulum of peace" doesn't swing to the intolerant extreme. We lean on your incredible practical stamina and value your tranquil solidity.

MAGENTA

(Range also includes Fuchia)

" I am charming, and make my fantasies my reality!"

Configurations

7◆4■1●	
8◆4■	See Red for Flashes
8◆3■1●	See Red for Blend
8◆2●2■	See Salmon for Blend
8◆2■2●	See Salmon for Blend
6◆4■2●	See Salmon for Flashes
6◆3●3■	See Plum for Blend
6◆3■3●	See Plum for Blend

Magenta Personality Profile

Associated with Earth Combustion mixing with Air Travel, Magenta describes *Imagination and Movement.*

Blending Primary Red with Primary Blue, Secondary Purple is created. Red is again added into the mix, resulting in vibrant high-keyed Magenta.

The great escapist, Magenta, you can make an exit faster than Harry Houdini. Blending Red Earth Combustion with Blue Air Travel, you are constantly on the move. And, you do *love to travel.* Tuned to momentary pleasures, you *cherish your freedom.* Rarely seen with a suntan, you don't sit still long enough to "soak up the rays."

You are carefree, yet sensitive. "Untouchable" like the fairy in Peter Pan, you are whimsical, hopeful and have a definite flair.

Dreamy, you are highly interested in space travel and psychic phenomenon. This is only natural, since you are without a doubt, *psychic*.

Pleasant surprises are a particular delight to you, especially those enlightening experiences that buoy up your existence and let in "a breath of fresh air"--anything that will ease and help you to cope with the mundane banalities of everyday living.

A powerful color very *open to new ideas and experiences*, Magenta you are more *spontaneous* than a flash of Turquoise. Highly *magnetic*, you attract friends who like to loosen up and need to dream a little. Very at ease around Blues, they comfort you day to day and help to guide you through the confusions of here-and-now reality.

Gracious, you *enjoy being with and working with people*. Frequently the "host or hostess with the mostest", you may chose a career in restaurant or hotel catering. You also gravitate to areas of entertainment, the theater and the arts, to travel, and can be very successful in sales.

PLUM

(Range includes Burgundy, Wine, Grape and Maroon)

"I am kind, warm, sensual and sincere. Enjoying dignity and ceremony, I can also be very jovial and talkative."

Configurations

5◆4■3●

7◆3■2● See Magenta for Flashes

6◆3●3■ See Magenta for Blend

6◆3■3● See Magenta for Blend

5◆5■2● See Salmon for Flashes

5■5◆2● See Salmon for Flashes

Plum Personality Profile

Earthly Energy Reflected through the Air (Purple) when stabilized by Brown (Fixed Stable Energy), allows Plum, *Spiritual Earth Force, to emerge.*

When Primary Red and Blue combine to form Purple, then a little drop of Red, some Yellow and a bit of Blue are carefully added into the Red-Blue Blend, we "pull out a Perfect Plum".

PLummmmmmmm.......just savor the luscious hummmmm. Sincere and sensual, warm and passionate, you are the most earthy of the Purples. Blending Brown into your physical and spiritual balance, you add stabilizing weight to your energy. Just the sound of your name brings ripe visions of sweet juiciness.

Your generally happy, jovial and talkative nature makes you a "peach" of a pal, and friendship is of ultimate value to you. But, equally dignified, you are a very good listener, an intuitive, concerned and compassionate friend.

Artistic, you love to be in the limelight. Sociable, you are a gracious host or hostess.

Plum, you are involved and courageous. Your beliefs are yours. You stand behind your ideals without fear of being ostracized. And, just for a special dash of Plum prestidigitation, you can magically project "pet dreams" into material maturation.

You enjoy children, offering them an attentive ear and kindness. You also enjoy ritualistic "pomp and circumstance".

Balance all of your wonderful attributes, Plum, and avoid extremes. Make sure your "pomp" isn't pompous, your compassionate concern steers clear of maudlin and your strong beliefs avoid self-righteousness. You have always been and continue to be a creative comfort to your colorful colleagues.

BROWN

(Range includes Medium to Dark Browns, Chocolate, Sepia, Bark and Dark Cocoa)

"I am hard working, enduring, solid and substantial!"

Configurations

6■3●3◆

6■3◆3●

5●4◆3■ See Chartreuse for Flashes

Brown Personality Profile

Associated with the Three Primary Energies, Mental, Physical and Spiritual, Brown describes *Stable Fixed Energy.*

Blending the Three Primaries, Red, Yellow and Blue, Brown is born.

Like the preponderant Sequoias, Brown, you are the solid and substantial, practical and proud pillar of our multi-hued society. Combining the Primaries, Red, Yellow and Blue, you are Fixed Stable Earth-richness.

More than a good provider who relates well to the physical and material, you enjoy being leaned on. And, though generally surrounding yourself with the practical and the functional, you can also be very sensual, taking great pleasure and luxuriating in the sultry.

Dominant, like the redwoods, you are strong and very definite in your dealings with people, insisting on a firm hold in every situation. Ambitious, you can be a leader. Hard working, you can handle tedium. But, beware, "definite" *can turn to* "domineering", "firm hold" to "unyielding prejudice" and "ambition" to "total materialism".

You respect tradition, are wary of change and do not accept "flack" in a relationship. Very competitive, you can be excellent in business, sports, politics, accounting and finance. You do not take financial risks, but rather gravitate to a secure and solid company where you prefer to work as part of a dignified team.

Staunch and stalwart, you sustain us, revitalizing and enriching our Planetary Palette.

PROFILES IN BRIEF

Beige

"Usually"	*"Can also be"*
Respectful	Lacking in spontaneity
Bright	Frustratingly noncommittal
Refined	Too strategic
Balanced	Too subdued
Confident	Too conservative
Firm in action and beliefs	Overly dry
Self-appreciative	A "stickler to the rules"
Sophisticated	
Philosophical	
Neutral, but strong	
Conservative	
Subdued	
Purposeful with firm foothold	
Blends with environment	
Directs behind the scenes	

Blue

"Usually"	*"Can also be"*
Enduring	Plodding
Spiritual	Passive
Intense	Flighty
Even	Slow
Quiet	Easily disoriented if shocked
Subtle	Clinging
Powerful	Submissive
Mysteriously seductive	Melancholy
Intuitive	Picky, fastidious
Sensitive	Neurotic
Sentimental	A muller, dwelling on one thing
Strong-willed	Pious
Fair	
Kind	
Artistic, poetic, musical	
Comforting	
An appreciator of beauty	
Serene	

"Usually"	*"Can also be"*

Brown

"Usually"	*"Can also be"*
Physical	Domineering
Material	Materialistic
Part of the crowd	Too ambitious
Functional and substantial	Unyielding
Rich, solid	Closed-minded
Definite in ideas	Unchangeable
Strong	Prejudiced
One who can be leaned on	
Competitive	
Hard-working	
Proud	
Traditional	
Dignified	
A pillar of society	
A good provider	
Good in business, finance	
Good in sports	
Not a financial risk-taker	
Good in handling tedium	

Chartreuse

"Usually"	*"Can also be"*
Modern	Introverted in personal life
Electric	Explosive when confused
Seeks stimulation	Hyper
Forward-looking	An avoider of intimate relationships
Looks for excitement	
Active	
A lover of clarity	
A lover of crisp thought	
Open to new thought, ideas	
Avant garde	
Full of life	
Inventive	
An active thinker	
Bright	
A "try anything once" person	

"Usually"	*"Can also be"*

Canteloupe

"Usually"

- Soft
- Lucid
- Charming
- Fluid in movement
- Strives to be gentle
- Philanthropic
- Youthfully beautiful
- Very generous
- Crowd shy
- Quietly strong
- (Often) *very* artistic
- Energetic
- A lover of money
- A lover of personal freedom
- Loves to be admired
- Romantic idealist
- "Feels" Non-physical (at times)
- Untouchable (in a way)

"Can also be"

- Careless
- Too Lucid
- Too Free
- Often insecure
- Fearful of future
- A social butterfly
- Easily lost in own world

Green

"Usually"

- Harmonious
- Peace-loving
- In tune with surroundings
- Moves "with the tide"
- Soft
- Methodical
- Giving
- Hopeful
- Strongly affected by environs
- Kind
- Creative in art, music, science
- Tries to get along with everyone
- Appreciates serenity
- Good at comprehending "things"
- Idealistic ("serenity" is ideal)

"Can also be"

- Reclusive
- Complacent
- Pessimistic
- Greedy
- Giving to a fault
- Depressed
- Hungry for recognition
- Heavy, easily putting on weight

"Usually"	"Can also be"
Indigo	
Powerful	Easily bored
Quiet	Loner
Determined	Too serious
Intuitive	Overly-sensitive
Psychic fascination with "past"	Too self-indulgent
Hard-working	
A keeper of secrets	
Non-conformist (many times)	
Looks easy-going, but is not	
Thorough	
A good researcher	
Religious (but self-styled)	
Trustworthy	
A very good friend	
A wise counsellor	
Fascinated by the unknown	
A lover of beauty	
A lover of the Universe	
Lavender	
Dreamy	Very pessimistic
Hopeful	Insecure
(hopes to be optimistic)	Fearful of strong passion
Spiritual	Often overtaken by sadness
Strives to be thoughtful	Impractical
Romantic	Unstable
Is looking for a happy ending	Over-emotional
Sentimental	Easily changeable
Strong-minded when positive	
A lover of beauty	
Inspired	
Quiet	
Sympathetic	
Very traditional (Often)	
Strives to be a free spirit	

	"Usually"	"Can also be"
Magenta	Highly magnetic A lover of travel Psychic A personality with flair Whimsical Loves "pleasant surprises" Sensitive Hopeful Dreamy Open to new ideas Loves *self*-freedom Spontaneous Always on the move Carefree Comfortable around "Blues" Will do something "for a lark" Flexible	Escapist Easily changeable Attractive to unproductive dreamers Tuned to momentary pleasures Easily confused Too flexible Unrealistic (difficulty dealing with reality) Untouchable Unfocused, lacking concentration) Freewheeling
Olive	Practical, Hard-working Traditional Intelligent Very realistic Hopeful (but not a dreamer) Appreciates the exotic Sympathetic Appreciates peace Does not like "waves" Solid, enduring Open-minded to others One who can be leaned on Strong, with great stamina Accepting of others, but will not be modified Goes with pragmatic norm	Plodding Set in ways Subdued Entrenched Sometimes too safe

"Usually"	"Can also be"

Orange

"Usually"	"Can also be"
A comfort-lover	Fickle
Social	changing commitments
A leader	with ease
Strives for simplicity of thought	A rationalizer
Hard-working	Materialistic
Ambitious, Goal oriented	Selfish
Energetic	Overly proud
Happy	Not very "deep"
A "center stage" personality	Superficially involved
Practical	
Earthy	
Athletic, Relates well physically	
Proud	
A lover of facts	
An organizer	
Enthusiastic	
A driving force	
Happy working with people	
Loves "causes"	

Plum

"Usually"	"Can also be"
Kind	Pompous
Warm	Ritualistic
Sincere	Maudlin
Sociable	Self-righteous
A good host or hostess	Condescending
A good listener	Over-sympathetic
Artistic, Intuitive	
Sensual	
Compassionate	
Enjoys children	
Hard-working	
Concerned, involved	
Dignified	
Stands up for beliefs	
Passionate, feeling	

	"Usually"	"Can also be"
Purple		
	Intuitive	A power-lover
	Fascinating	A control "freak"
	Fascinated with "things"	Fussy
	Artistic, Musical, Poetic	Too egocentric
	A creative thinker	Neurotic
	Spiritual	Melancholy
	Easily affected by emotions of others	Opinionated
	Avant garde in thought	A snob
	Strong-willed	
	Intellectual	
	Free-thinking	
	Dynamic	
	Powerful	
	Majestic	
	Sensitive	
	Individualistic, prefers to "make own way"	
	Respectful of knowledge	
Red		
	Dynamic, Energy giver	Impatient
	Powerful, Intense	Fickle if bored
	Fast-paced	Extremely anxious
	Warm, Physical	Egocentric
	Exciting	Exhausted (intense energy, is not durable)
	Passionate	Changeable (changes commitments without looking back
	Competitive	Insensitive to other's needs
	A winner	
	Needs to be noticed	
	Enthusiastic	
	Independent	
	Challenging	
	Positive	
	Purposeful	

"Usually"	"Can also be"

Salmon

"Usually"	"Can also be"
"Bright idea" personality	Overly possessive
Alert	Overly demanding
Sensuous	Too questioning
A good communicator	Condescending
Enthusiastic	Bossy
Seems "Bigger than Life!"	"Busy body"
Energetic	A show-off
Curious	A snob
Hard-working	
Leader, but not forerunner	
Astounding likes to amaze people	
Prefers to be boss, but... works well *for* someone	
Warm, friendly	

Turquoise

"Usually"	"Can also be"
Spontaneous	Indecisive
A lover of change	Confused
An explorer	Easily changeable (regarding commitments)
A seeker of knowledge	Lost in own projected image
Hopeful	Selfish (too busy with image)
Open	
Accepting of new ideas, situations	
Independent	
Chameleon-like (changes appearance)	
Gracious	
Exciting	
Fun	
Makes commitments	
Solid	
Purposeful (always a reason for changes, transitions)	

	"Usually"	"Can also be"
Yellow		
	Athletic	Uncertain of actions
	Warm	Compulsive
	Searching	*Unaware* of actions
	Strong	Prejudiced
	Fast-paced	Myopic (wanting to see things his or her own way)
	Electric	Irrational
	Very rational	Sporadic
	Energetic	A "stumbler" (searches without knowing what for; "stumbles over" what is found)
	Open	
	Scientific	
	Intelligent	
	Fun-loving	
	Ambitious	
	Bright	

YOUR MAGNETIC ATTRACTIONS

Friendships, Affairs, Romance, Business

You, individually, are the most vital, primary force in your universe. Your basic magnetic energy field dictates what you will "attract" into your personal world, and also, influences what you will find attractive.

A curious and tricky business this phenomenon called magnetism--this mysterious force that can unfold a forever friendship, motion us toward a business ally, subtly sweep us into sweet romance or hurl us headlong into a torrid affair. Repulsion, itself, can be powerfully magnetic. The push and pull of currents can gather such an irresistible surge, that the force can flip us midair and we find ourselves flying feet first into a relationship with someone who initially made us *see red.* A curious and very tricky energy, indeed.

There are a myriad of reasons why, and many ways in which, colors gravitate to each other. So, knowing that the exception may prove the rule, let's take a look at your most workable bets, your most vital and intense attractions in *friendships, love affairs, enduring romances and business associations* based on your Colorsope--*the individual-basic-energy-you!*

RED

Red you attract everyone, what more can we say!

Friendships

A very strong personality, Red, only another very very strong personality can weather your energy, enthusiasm and drive.

Blue. The intense you is balanced by Blue, another Primary hue. Both heavy weights, you sense each other's needs and counter each other's basic energies. A winning combination, you can work as an affair, marriage and/or business association.

Yellow. Joining your vitality with explosive Yellow makes for a friendship that's ready for excitement and new projects. This can include romance and a possible business venture--a vital partnership that can accomplish much.

Red. Red, your self-love is reflected in your many Red friends who mirror all the qualities you so enjoy in yourself. Comfortable with yourself anywhere, your many Red friends can appear in love or in business.

Beige. Beige can also work across the board. You both deeply respect each other's independence.

Magenta. For a friendship that is amusing, entertaining and filled with "flair", try Magenta. Highly magnetic, the two of you will live in a whirlwind.

Chartreuse. An innovative and exciting friendship is shared with Chartreuse.

Indigo. Intense and passionate, your investigative nature is fulfilled in your close association with Indigo, another detective who likes the facts!

Turquoise. Red, you and Turquoise, independent souls that you are, spend many hours seeking fun, excitement and knowledge--an innovative combination that might find business a lucrative association.

Canteloupe. "Limelight Lovers", you and Canteloupe have fabulous fun times.

Salmon. Another "Limelight Lover", Salmon joins in. Communicative and social, you quickly move on to an exciting, passionate affair.

Purple. Equally intense and powerful, Red and Purple combine in a creative, free-thinking friendship that can continue as lasting love and/or a vital business association.

Brief Affairs

Red, you can have an affair with anyone–not that you always, or even usually, do. It's just that you are so interested in so many things and so many people without expecting much in return that you actually can have a brief, loving interlude with most any color.

By no means promiscuous, you are very selective. Any affair you might have had, or any that you might entertain in the future, is, and will be sincere! You mean everything you do!

If you are curious (of course you are) sneak a peek at "Brief Affairs" under the other colors to see how you did!

Enduring Romances

Your enduring romances are always intense, vital, fast-moving and forward-looking.

Brown. A good bet for enduring romance is proud, solid, substantial, earthy Brown. You work very well together--enduring in love and even business.

Red. Another Red who shares your passion, love of life and who understands your nature, can excite across the board--friend, lover and business associate.

Orange. Vital Orange is another winner. Earthy, passionate and exciting, you both respect each other's individuality.

Blue. Blue balances you. You fulfill each other's needs on spiritual and physical levels.

Plum. Mutually respectful individuals with a purpose, you and Plum find enduring love.

Purple. Exceedingly powerful, Red and Purple endure in an intense, creative and passionate association.

Beige. Very interested in the self-fulfillment of one another, a Beige love builds an enduring romance on individual independence.

Olive. Allowing you the freedom you cherish, you excite Olive with your accomplishments. Inspiring Olive, you give the utmost respect in return--a good foundation for lasting commitment.

Yellow. Red/Yellow combine in a definite maybe. Both strong Primaries, you work well as friends, business associates and lovers, but an enduring romance works best only if you share the same goals.

Salmon. A Red/Salmon romance continues volatile and intense--and you love it!

Business Associations

Strong and determined, Red, you can cut short any partnership that's weak, non-productive or boring. You need to succeed!

Purple. Intense, powerful, creative free-thinkers, ready for new ideas, give you and Purple an upper hand in business.

Beige. Hard-driving Beige and Red combine well in a single goal.

Brown. Materialistic and ambitious Brown balances Red--a lucrative combination.

Salmon. Hard-working enthusiastic showmen with endless energy, Salmon and Red drive through until the job is done.

Turquoise. Red and Turquoise, a fabulously exciting business combination--innovative, fast-paced and expansive.

Indigo. Solid and powerful, Indigo and Red could build an empire together.

Red. Red/Red is a fast-moving, risk-taking, competitive combo that wins. *They insist on it!*

Blue. A well-balanced, sound, business association is blended with Blue.

Yellow. The high-energy of Yellow in concert with Red accomplishes much.

Olive. Olive and Red combine in an innovative, constructive association.

Orange. Sturdy and directed, Red and Orange join for profit and gain.

YELLOW

Yellow, you attract intellectuals, ambitious people, fun-lovers and those needing energy!

Friendships

Lavender. A friendship with Lavender is investigative. Both flying a little higher than the earth, you'll have great fun "uncovering things" together. All things in order, your friendship could blossom into a light and fun affair.

Indigo. Allied with another seeker of knowledge, you and Indigo strike an intellectual friendship that could develop very deep feelings for each other.

Blue. In a friendship of exchange, Blue will calm you, and you will energize Blue.

Turquoise. Turquoise provides you with an exciting and active friendship that can fan the flames of enduring romance.

Green. A solid bet. You enjoy Green. A stable enduring relationship can go from pal, to affair, to lasting romance.

Chartreuse. An exciting whirlwind meeting with Chartreuse can carry you all the way, business, romance, the works!

Red. Feisty, exciting and forward-looking Red provides you with the same opportunities as Chartreuse--but with a very different tempo.

Yellow. Of course, Yellow befriending Yellow makes for an enduring relationship, all else accounted for, romance may be in order.

Purple. An intellectual and spiritual friendship with Purple remains just that. No wedding bells here, usually!

Canteloupe. Sweet and light, you find a friend and--the good possibility of a lover.

Orange. From a vibrant, vital, enthusiastic and energetic friendship, Orange may emerge as a business associate, significant other, and/or lover--every bit of it *very exciting!*

Brown. From a very stable and substantial friendship, you and Brown may well decide to go into business together.

Brief Affairs

Yellow, so many of your friendships can turn into delightful affairs, and so many of your lovers can wind up as lasting friends.

Lavender. Light and fun, Lavender can be a lovely intermezzo.

Indigo, on the other hand, could almost immediately unfold an enduring and meaningful romance.

Blue. Your easy balance with Blue finds a lover and a friend. From two different worlds, you both give equally.

Turquoise. Exotic and fun, you may find a flash of Turquoise in your love life.

Green. A peaceful and tranquil affair may give you a refreshing friend in Green--and an enduring helpmate.

Chartreuse. Erratic and exciting, your Chartreuse affair is easily entertaining enough to last.

Red. Red gives you physical and intellectual stimulation that satisfies. Sharing the same goals, you move to the lasting romance category.

Canteloupe. From a lovely and inspiring affair, Canteloupe can also spell lasting *r-o-m-a-n-c-e.*

Yellow. Yellow and Yellow move from a very thought-out affair to a very planned and enduring romance.

Orange. From a burst of energy and excitement, you and Orange continue with a very challenging commitment.

Olive. An enduring relationship blossoms from a very serious and rational affair with Olive.

Salmon. Caught up in a material and intellectual "blast", you and Salmon enjoy a brief sequence that, surprisingly, generates lasting love.

Enduring Romances

Green. Yellow, your romance with Green offers refreshing peace and tranquility, a fulfilling love that can well endure.

Chartreuse. Innovative Chartreuse will keep love electric and exciting, providing you with all the intellectual stimulation you need.

Red. You'll never go hunting with Red energy around--not only intellectually, but physically exciting.

Canteloupe. Light, warm and rich, you bask in lasting romance with Canteloupe.

Orange. An exciting, energetic and purposeful love-life is enjoyed with Orange.

Olive. With Olive you find solidity and respectability.

Yellow. Yellow offers a rational, intellectually energizing romance.

Indigo. With Indigo, you stay strong and purposeful in love.

Salmon. Filled with many surprises, a whirlwind affair with Salmon endures. Nurtured through mind and matter, material and intellectual interests thrive.

Business Associations

Yellow, your best business associations are:

Blue. Solid and open-minded.

Chartreuse. Innovative and exciting.

Red. Great at developing an idea into a finished product.

Orange. A hard-working side-by-side partner.

Olive. Provides a solid and stable working relationship.

Brown. Functional, will work with you in a preestablished pattern, such as a franchise, to a very lucrative result.

Green. Offers a very rational, intellectual association.

BLUE

Blue, you attract someone looking for solid comfort!

Friendships

A very friendly color, Blue, most any color blends with "hue". Not unlike Green, who is, after all, half Blue, you have many friends who come to you for advice, serenity and a Spiritual lift.

Brief Affairs

Blue, your affairs are kind and loving. No one can ever question your sincerity.

Red. All at once calming, soothing and exciting, Red and Blue see-saw in a critical balance as opposites attract. Both strong Primaries, the affair can continue.

Blue. Deep understanding friendship offers Blue and Blue a chance at lasting Love.

Yellow. Adding energy to tranquilizing Blue, Yellow entertains a brief interlude.

Magenta. Exciting and creative, lively and searching, an episode with Magenta can move to solid ground.

Purple. Spiritually powerful, and perhaps brief, but odds are that Purple and Blue will move across the board--friends, lovers and business associates.

Indigo. Intense and soulful, a terse mysterious interlude with Indigo will echo in your dreams for years.

Turquoise. Totally enjoyable and constantly different, an ever-changing Turquoise/Blue affair entertains a good chance at lasting commitment.

Green. Loving and gentle, a meeting with Green can go for the works--sympathetic lovers can grow to enduring commitment, a friendship and/or a working relationship.

Beige. Subtle and sophisticated, "briefly" Beige *turns to a total tuning in.* We hear wedding bells here.

Canteloupe. To all appearances, your Canteloupe affair will be light, but surprise--a sincere and feeling relationship grows!

Olive. A low-key episode with Olive goes for solid commitment.

Lavender. A spiritual "splash" with romantic Lavender quickly forms deep refreshing pools of consideration.

Chartreuse. Stimulating and refreshing Chartreuse and Blue balance in a progressive commitment.

Plum. Spiritual and loving, an affair with Plum is almost never brief.

Enduring Romances

Your romances, Blue, endure—rich, spiritual and solid!

Red. Balancing well physically and intellectually, a Red/Blue love moves to an exciting, passionate and satisfying commitment.

Blue. With deep concern for each other's needs, a Blue/Blue affair quietly blossoms into loving romance.

Magenta. Excitingly creative, lively and entertaining, your Magenta love endures with compassion.

Purple. Strong emotional and spiritual ties are the key in a Purple/Blue match.

Turquoise. Panoramic entertainment is slated for Blue and Turquoise as long as you remember to respect each other's freedom.

Green. Loving and fruitful, considerate and sympathetic, Green and Blue go hand-in-hand in an enduring romance.

Beige. With respect for each other's life-style, Beige and Blue continue to grow.

Canteloupe. Forever titillating, Blue loves the charm and gentility of Canteloupe, and Canteloupe melts under Blue's powerful subtle energy.

Lavender. Spiritually oriented, Lavender and Blue are eternally interested in each other's well-being.

Olive. Low-keyed and solid, Olive and Blue quietly grow to depend on each other.

Plum. A lively affair with Plum develops into a passionate enduring romance.

Chartreuse. Inventive and vital, Chartreuse continues to infuse Blue with new free-thinking ideas, while Blue offers Chartreuse a stable base of operation.

Business Associations

Blue, your associates find you trusting, sincere and reliable.

Red. Different perspectives view the entire "ball park" in a rich Red/Blue alliance.

Blue. Durable Blue and Blue work well together.

Yellow. Yellow creatively and intellectually supports Blue's concepts in a solid working relationship.

Purple. Definite in your actions, Purple and you combine in a very strong, solid and dependable partnership.

Green. In a Blue/Green operation, Blue holds down the fort, while Green is up-front. Both are able to dream a little and bring their ideas to fruition through hard work--and you are both hard-workers!.

Canteloupe. Canteloupe and Blue make a charming, exciting, trusting, well-balanced team.

Olive. Similar energies unite Blue and Olive in a practical, solid, goal-oriented partnership.

Salmon. Another good balance is struck when Blue and Salmon combine. Creative and aware of subtle nuances, this team can find business very lucrative!

ORANGE

Very magnetic, Orange, you can attract leaders and ambitious people–an "Orange" woman could, in fact, captivate a very powerful man. Exciting and fun, you attract social people and people who are looking to become more social. Physically oriented comfort-lovers are also drawn by your magnetism. And, strange as it seems, there are times when the insecure and timid seek comfort in your energy and safety.

Friendships

Turquoise. Orange, you love new ideas. Not only do you find a creative friend in Turquoise, but a fun and vital relationship that can run the gamut--love affair, lasting romance and business ally.

Purple. Power meets power in an association based on analytical temperaments--your Purple pal can turn to *purple passion,* lasting romance and even business ventures.

Plum. Warm and caring, an alliance with Plum can eventually mean financial enterprise.

Yellow. Orange and Yellow blend in an exciting, energetic and purposeful friendship.

Canteloupe. Relaxation comes to the fore in a casual surface association with Canteloupe.

Orange. Orange meets Orange to go across the board--energetic fast-paced friendship and affair, enduring romance and bustling business.

Salmon. Both showmen, Orange and Salmon do fabulously well socially, and you might even decide to make the alliance permanent.

Brown. A practical and thoughtful friendship is enjoyed with Brown.

Olive. A rational and compatible association with Olive can lead to an affair or business relationship.

Chartreuse. An easy, warm and creative friendship with Chartreuse moves to an exciting affair.

Brief Affairs

Turquoise. Fast-paced and goal-oriented, you and Turquoise go for a "spin"!

Chartreuse. A momentary flash of excitement is provided by Chartreuse.

Purple. Physically strong and passionate, your affair with Purple continues in enduring intimacy.

Green. Well matched physically and intellectually, Orange and Green balance each other's "feelings"--a good chance, here, for enduring romance.

Red. A "wow!" of an affair that doesn't have to end--vital, creative and exciting as the energies of Red and Orange blend.

Orange. Another winner as Orange and Orange go strong!

Salmon. Active and responsive, highly emotional and possessive, when Salmon and Orange get started, "don't *nobody* get in the way!"

Olive. More excitement as Orange and Olive progress to deep understanding and affection.

Magenta. Barometric and carefree, a high-flying Magenta/Orange affair has a soaring chance at lasting success.

Yellow. Bursting with excitement and energy, a Yellow affair just "happens".

Canteloupe. A casual relaxing friendly affair grows in fertile fields to a rich, warm materialistic alliance.

Lavender. Dear warm, magnetic, Orange, though brief, there's a strong chance that a Lavender affair will make a dramatic appearance.

Enduring Romances

Turquoise. Similar energies grow together for a long-lasting, strong and loving commitment.

Purple. Intense and enduring, Orange and Purple intimacies ripen to a loving romance.

Green. Sensitive balance finds your Green affair maturing to a secure, lasting love.

Olive. Enduring respect and lasting romance is slated here.

Red. Perpetually percolating, Orange/Red continue into a romance that is more than warm and passionate.

Orange. An Orange/Orange affair finds growing deep respect for mutual feelings and well-being.

Salmon. Ongoing and intense, your relationship with Salmon is exciting. Social and material interests in common, finds you both developing many new avenues together.

Magenta. An exciting and energetic love progresses from an erratic and carefree affair.

Yellow. With all the energy and excitement of the "initial happening", your Yellow/Orange affair continues into purposeful love.

Canteloupe. A lasting commitment grows from love and friendship.

Business Associations

Purple. A very good business balance is offered by Purple; your minds work very positively together.

Turquoise. In an Orange/Turquoise alliance, a forceful, durable, strong and exciting team is created.

Green. An Orange/Green business combo is a great bet in a franchise operation--you respect each other's abilities and plan well together.

Chartreuse. Volatile and creative, a Chartreuse/Orange endeavor is very fruitful indeed.

Plum. A creative, solid and lucrative business can be formed by Orange and Plum.

Orange. Orange/Orange spells a whirlwind of activity, working well in a "hopping" relationship.

Salmon. Both real showman, like everything else you undertake with Salmon, business is exciting.

Olive. A strong business force combines in an Olive/ Orange merger.

Brown. Like Olive, Brown/Orange are "loaded for bear" in business.

Beige. An Orange/Beige combo brings excitement with financial rewards.

Red. Directed sturdy energies, Red and Orange join forces for profit and gain.

Yellow. Yellow working side by side with Yellow forms a hard-driving business team.

Canteloupe. And a lively and exciting materialistic partnership is struck with Yellow and Canteloupe.

GREEN

Green, you attract those who seek peace and harmony!

Friendships

Green, harmonious Green, you strive to be generous with everyone. Too numerous to mention, your kind and giving nature is reflected in your many close and loving friends.

Brief Affairs

Indeed, very few of your romances are brief, Green. Like your friendships, your affairs unfold enduring loving relationships. The few exceptions include Magenta, Plum and Salmon.

Magenta. A Magenta/Green lively and carefree episode remains just that.

Plum. Lively and humorous, you and Plum enjoy an interlude. Very protective of each other, you decide to keep it light.

Salmon. Intrigued by Salmon, Orange, likewise, fascinates Salmon, but your views on life differ too widely. Not enough in common, the affair is bewitchingly brief.

Enduring Romances

Blue. A loving and sincere Blue/Green affair blossoms into a warm and caring romance.

Yellow. In a sunny episode, Yellow picks up your pace, while you offer Yellow tranquility. Refreshing and enduring love continues for both.

Canteloupe. Exciting, intellectual and good-natured, Green/Canteloupe unfold a lasting love with an erratic tempo.

Orange. Stimulating and creative, Orange and Green strike a good balance. A progressive duo, this love endures.

Olive. With philosophies, "ideas" and strategies in common, an exciting beginning goes on to a lasting Olive/Green Love.

Caring, but slow-moving, romance with **Brown** lumbers on to heavy, solid, satisfying commitment.

Salmon. Green and Salmon move from a physical, passionate and caring affair to a dignified, respectful and passionate love.

Lavender. Lavender adds a touch of "fairy dust" to a loving relationship with Green that remains forever hopeful.

Indigo. Friendly and sincere an Indigo/Green meeting moves to passionate, intense and exciting... and what's more, it lasts!

Business Associations

Very dependable Green, you get the job done!

Blue. A Blue/Green partnership works comfortably in a creative venture.

Yellow. Based on intellectualism, a Yellow/Green association is strictly rational.

Canteloupe. Exciting and mellow in your approach to people, a Canteloupe/Green enterprise best deals directly with the public.

Orange. Open-minded and secure in their association, Orange/Green are very progressive partners that plan well together.

Salmon. Salmon and Green find themselves in a very stimulating venture.

Olive. Deep down practicality draw Olive and Green together.

Brown. In a solid and rich exchange, Green and Brown are in it "for the bread"!

PURPLE

Attracting artists, intellectuals and opinionated free-thinkers, you repel sceptics and those who are fearful. Powerful Purple, be assured, you will draw nothing but the strong to your side!

Friendships

Strong-willed Purple, you are a sincere and serious friend.

Green. A mutual understanding with Green is honest and rich.

Red. Majestically intense and equally powerful, Red joins you in a creative free-thinking union that can expand to fill any area of your life, be it an affair, enduring love, or successful business.

Blue. Spiritually oriented, you share philosophies with Blue--a deep friendship evolves.

Yellow. Primary and powerful Yellow offers spiritual and intellectual camaraderie.

Orange. A commanding friendship based on analytical temperaments magnetizes Orange and Purple into an enduring relationship.

Brown. Brown joins Purple in a very practical, very solid association--no lightweight friendship this.

Purple. Purple meets Purple in an abundant and vital give-and-take friendship based on mutual interests.

Indigo. Strong and intense, Purple and Indigo share an obsession to unveil mysteries and secrets.

Lavender. On a lighter side, Lavender, sparkling with new thoughts and a change of pace, charms you in an enlightening and delightful association.

Brief Affairs and Enduring Romances

Purple, you are too intense for many brief encounters. After a "taste of honey", it's *all or nothing* with you!

Magenta. An uninhibited, passionate interlude with Magenta instantly moves to free-thinking romance with loving consideration.

Red. Red and Purple, intense, explosive and exciting, start out like the Fourth of July and stay that way. Both fuel the flames of passion.

Blue. A very serious beginning with Blue, quickly moves into deeply felt romance.

Plum. Irresistibly compelled by Plum, differing natures make this short affair intensely emotional.

Brown. Exciting, solid and practical, Brown and Purple unfold an enduring romance.

Orange. Off to a passionate and physical beginning, a Purple/Orange affair rapidly develops deep mutual respect for each other's feelings and well-being.

Purple. A hopeful, positive and strong alliance from the start, Purple and Purple move to a deep-feeling lasting relationship.

Chartreuse. Innovative and exciting, an affair based on *ideas and thoughts* finds you and Chartreuse deeply enmeshed in a strong-willed, free-thinking modern romance.

Indigo. Compelling and intense, an affair with Indigo unfolds a smoldering love with the rare quality of deep understanding.

Turquoise. A very light, fun affair with Turquoise may surprise you and develop into a sincere and solid commitment.

Business Associations

Purple, your business associations can fulfill your dreams of power!

Indigo. An Indigo and Purple partnership is strong, powerful and positive in its goals.

Beige. A Beige/Purple combo forms a durable driving force with the ability to placate each other--a very lucrative proposition.

Red. Red and Purple find an association that is intense, powerful, free-thinking and ready for new ideas.

Brown. Very practical, Brown and Purple combine in a strong and directed force.

Plum. Differing viewpoints "rub" in a progressive association with Purple and Plum.

Chartreuse. An innovative, fast-paced business relationship.

Blue. Solid, understanding, compatible partners, Purple and Blue collaborate well.

Salmon. A creative, hard-driving team, you and Salmon accomplish what most think impossible.

Olive. Olive offers solid support as you seek new avenues for business.

Orange. Orange/Purple, a very good business balance, work positively together.

CANTELOUPE

A soft subtle color, Canteloupe, you attract soft loving people.

Friendships

A loving and caring friend, you generally prefer light, fun friendships.

Red. Similar interests draw Canteloupe and Red together for a taste of adventure. Exciting and materialistic, you'll find yourselves forever delving into "fun things".

Lavender. An airy easy friendship with dreamy Lavender may blossom into a sweet affair with wedding bells in the offing.

Magenta. Another light and breezy friendship may take you and Magenta into an enduring love.

Orange. Canteloupe and Orange can relax in what appears to be a warm surface friendship.

Plum. Very socially oriented, your Plum chum and you may be in for some pleasant surprises. Quickly encompassed by deep loving emotion, you may consider a permanent alliance.

Chartreuse. "Electrically charged" Chartreuse offers you a most creative friendship.

Blue. A spiritually oriented association with Blue might take you around all the bases--friendship, marriage and business.

Canteloupe. A very, very light wispy Canteloupe friendship can waft through an airy affair right into a successful business venture.

Yellow. Light and sweet, a friendship with Yellow can move across the board--lover, friend and business associate.

Brief Affairs

Magenta. Gentle and generous, an interlude with Magenta unfolds lasting romance.

Salmon. With Salmon there is fun, flicker, flash and out!

Lavender. Sweet, docile and romantic, your Lavender affair continues on to lasting romance.

Plum. Meaningful and intense, a Plum interlude provokes much more.

Canteloupe. Similar goals bring Canteloupe and Canteloupe together for a brief romantic episode, but taking another turn, you just might do some business together.

Beige. Sophisticated and elegant, your affair with Beige might well be catered. Lucky you, it continues!

Olive. Free, fascinating and solid, your Olive love is bound for more.

Green. With Green, a good-natured loving affair surveys matrimony.

Blue. A sincere and feeling Blue encounter can unfold in many directions--friendship, romance and/or business.

Orange. Rich and materialistic, a warm touch of Orange sows fertile seeds for business or marriage.

Chartreuse. A sensitive affair with Chartreuse finds you tuned to each other's needs.

Turquoise. Both seekers of beauty, Canteloupe and Turquoise begin a lovely romance filled with aspirations.

Indigo. A loving hopeful affair with Indigo quickly ends.

Yellow. A sunny warm Yellow/Canteloupe alliance looks like it will last.

Enduring Romances

Plum. From an intense and meaningful affair, your Plum romance endures with deep loving emotion.

Green. Exciting, intellectual and good-natured, love with an erratic tempo continues with Green.

Blue. An uplifting, spiritual relationship with Blue develops mutual lasting trust and interdependence.

Lavender. Respectful and romantic, a Lavender love continues to grow.

Orange. Fertile seeds planted in friendship and love come to fruition in an enduring romance with Orange.

Olive. An affair with Olive fast turns to a well-balanced love life. You fascinate Olive who provides you with the security, freedom and admiration you need.

Chartreuse. Warm and lively, Canteloupe and Chartreuse continue lovingly tuned to each other.

Turquoise. You and Turquoise create you own fairy tale romance.

Beige. Light and sensual, your Beige romance endures.

Magenta. Magenta and Canteloupe unfold mutual trust and dependency.

Yellow. From a lovely and inspiring affair, you continue to bathe in the sunny warmth of a Yellow romance.

Business Associations

Canteloupe, although you love money, you won't attempt a business venture unless you are sure that you will enjoy the time spent and the personal associations involved. Also, you must feel pride in the accomplishment, or it will not be worth the effort!

Blue. Canteloupe/Blue team up for a very good working balance and a solid trusting relationship.

Magenta. Active and exciting, Magenta and Canteloupe merge to produce a very creative, enterprising, "ready to take a chance" alliance.

Brown. A terrific balance is struck between Canteloupe and Brown. You both work different ends of the business, Canteloupe is the "idea person", Brown the practical partner. Canteloupe charms, Brown goes for "the kill"!

Beige. Another very enterprising combo emerges as Beige and Canteloupe, working well together, take on many creative challenges.

Orange. A very materialistic, lively and profitable partnership is shared by Canteloupe and Orange.

Canteloupe. Canteloupe and Canteloupe work well if both strive to bring their mutual dreams into practical working reality.

Chartreuse. A competitive team of free-thinkers is created in a Chartreuse/Canteloupe association. You both like to win!

Green. With Green, an exciting alliance is struck in an enterprise that deals directly with the public.

Indigo. Warm and industrious, an Indigo/Canteloupe partnership succeeds.

Lavender. By making other people's dreams come true, Canteloupe and Lavender financial aspirations become reality.

BEIGE

> ***Beige, you attract those who are bright, those who are hopeful of future assets, and those looking to be refined.***

Friendships

Beige, your friendships are tasteful, respectful, elegant and ceremonious.

Brown. Beige and Brown share similar ideals and enjoy a friendship of refined tastes.

Chartreuse. Erratic and fun, a lively friendship with Chartreuse keeps you hopping.

Lavender. Loving and gentle, Beige and Lavender could mean romance.

Red. An energetic, uncomplicated, materialistic alliance with Red can reach out to all facets of your life--friend, lover and business partner.

Plum. Very respectful, a Plum/Beige friendship is warm and feeling.

Indigo. Indigo shares a similar materialistic orientation. You discuss your philosophies of life.

Beige. Quite naturally, Beige and Beige enjoy each other's elegant tastes. You cultivate yourselves together, going to museums, concerts and the like.

Olive. An easy-going, secure, honest and trustworthy friendship with Olive pleases.

Salmon. Ceremonious, outgoing and social, Salmon and Beige combine for some fun.

Brief Affairs

Except for an interlude or two, Beige, you mean business. Very serious, as a rule, you are too deliberate to entertain anything frivolous or short-lived. Your "affairs" move to lasting commitment and enduring romance. But, still... there just might be one or two...

Canteloupe. Sensual Canteloupe just might seduce you into a light, reflective romance that could continue by the way!

Turquoise. Lively Turquoise can whirl you... but definitely... into a brief, modern, just-for-fun affair. Even the most serious of us have a few "lights" in the closet!

Enduring Romances

The friends you *so* enjoy may be the lovers you marry.

Brown. You wax elegant and eloquent in an affair with Brown; your intense, passionate and emotional romance endures.

Chartreuse. Effervescent, passionate and emotional a Chartreuse/Beige "love" of refined modern tastes and elegant appreciation is filled with surprises.

Lavender. Idealistic and hopeful, you enjoy a deep nurturing love with Lavender.

Red. Physically satisfying, your Red affair moves to a practical and dynamic commitment.

Plum. Very laid back, rich and sophisticated at the start, Plum and Beige endure in devoted trusting romance.

Indigo. An Indigo love--warm, dignified, sincere and passionate, is one of mutual admiration. Your love endures, honest and intense.

Beige. Ah! Beige and Beige, *the affair should definitely be catered!* Ceremonious in the extreme, it is elegance personified--but, it is also respectful and dignified, with deep honest enduring love.

Magenta. Lively, interesting and charming, you are very secure in your love with Magenta. You both are able to share your innermost feelings with each other.

Salmon. Humorous, playful and witty, you and Salmon allow each other the freedom you need. Trusting, physically satisfying, yet independent, you are always there for each other.

Canteloupe. Mutually agreed, that light, lovely affair with Canteloupe can continue sensually satisfying.

Blue. With deep respect for each other's way of life, Blue and Beige make a loving commitment.

Business Associations

Beige, no one need tell you this, but you can do business with anyone who is dependable. You are adaptable, creative and a directing force who does not allow personal feelings to interfere with business judgement-definitely a plus for anyone in business. Your need for and sense of achievement is so strong that it takes you to the top.

CHARTREUSE

> ***Highly electrical, Chartreuse, you attract all those ready for clear, bright avant garde thoughts.***

Friendships

Innovative and modem, you seek creative friendships.

Turquoise. An exciting choice is Turquoise. Your fast-moving friendship seeks out challenges.

Red. Red shares your love of activity in a very innovative, exciting association.

Yellow. An intellectual whirlwind of stimulation, with Yellow you can be carried straight into romance and, if you are so inclined, a business association.

Canteloupe. An electrically charged friendship with Canteloupe can also mean love and/or business.

Orange. Creative and lively, Orange meets Chartreuse in a friendship that could mean "affair".

Brown. Solid camaraderie is shared here.

Olive. Chartreuse and Olive balance--you stimulate and Olive "insulates".

Beige. A Beige influence calms. This friendship can go across the board--friendship, business, affair and enduring romance.

Plum. An understanding alliance with Plum kindles more than friendship.

Chartreuse. Of course, excitement sizzles as Chartreuse joins Chartreuse.

Brief Affairs

Barometric, your *"live-wire"* affairs *"crackle"!*

Red. Red is physical, innovative, exciting and whirlwind.

Chartreuse. Bright and inventive, Chartreuse "lights up" Chartreuse in a loving and lively affair. Sharing the same current, it looks like wedding bells here.

Yellow. Stimulation turns to high voltage excitement and Yellow and Chartreuse move to "affair".

Canteloupe. Loving, warm and sensitive, Canteloupe and Chartreuse "tune in".

Plum. Creative and loving, a Plum affair flows.

Orange. With Orange, lightning strikes, but the romance fizzles. You both love center-stage more.

Beige. Beige and Chartreuse team up for more than a "charge". You've got a lot going here!

Purple. Intense and searching, a Purple/Chartreuse affair is cleared for lasting love.

Lavender. Light, lovely, exciting and brief, the essence of a Lavender interlude lingers on.

Turquoise. Turquoise offers you an active affair with a pulsating panorama of just about everything. You find it energizing!

Blue. An understanding and undemanding affair with Blue is wired for romance,

Magenta. Your "Magenta moment" flashes light noncommittal fun.

Enduring Romances

Turquoise. An electric affair with Turquoise holds the promise of meaningful, sincere and lasting love.

Chartreuse. Compatible partners, Chartreuse and Chartreuse fuse in love and in business.

Yellow. Fun and exciting, Chartreuse and Yellow rationalize together. Forever seeking new avenues, your love remains bright.

Canteloupe. Continually tuned to each other's needs, Canteloupe and Chartreuse continue warm and affectionate.

Beige. An innovative, idea-loving modern romance is made with a partner that soothes. An alliance with lots of pluses--Beige provides a calming *circuit breaker* to boot!

Purple. A searching and intense affair "arcs" to a long-lasting, ever-growing romance with Purple.

Plum. There's a rich creative "current" in this love.

Blue. A wonderful affair with Blue unfolds a romance of self-fulfillment. There's deep caring here!

Business Associations

For you, Chartreuse, business must be fun and constantly changing!

Brown. Chartreuse and Brown work at different ends of the spectrum. Directed toward one goal, this proves to be an exciting creative association.

Orange. Barometric, your partnership with Orange will be volatile, but fruitful.

Purple. With Purple you will have a strong scientific orientation. Very creative!

Beige. Innovative, progressive thinkers, Chartreuse and Beige construct well together.

Chartreuse. Chartreuse and Chartreuse get an idea and "run" with it--a very industrious team.

Yellow. Chartreuse and Yellow are rational and directed.

Canteloupe. You and Canteloupe like to win--and you do!

Indigo. Solid pioneers, Indigo and Chartreuse can form a lucrative partnership.

Olive. A modern creative team that is able to deal with reality is formed in a Chartreuse/Olive combo.

Turquoise. A creative business with Turquoise will be fast-paced and electric!

TURQUOISE

Irresistibly drawn to your powerful magnet, Turquoise, you attract people with diverse interests.

Friendships

Explorers and seekers of many things **abound in your friendships.**

Red. Fast moving, inventive and eccentric, an *avant garde* alliance is quickly made with Red. Entertaining limelight-seekers, together you are a "super magnet" that really attracts a following.

Plum. Subjective personalities, Plum and Turquoise share opinions on matters of consequence--reviewing world affairs and the like.

Lavender. Outward appearances attract two dreamers. Lavender and Turquoise in a light, surface, casual friendship seem more like a three-ring circus.

Indigo. You amuse Indigo, while Indigo "grounds" you in a well-balanced, creative and sincere friendship.

Green. Light and fun, you strike up an easy association with Green.

Chartreuse. Chartreuse and Turquoise are forever "on the prowl", seeking challenge and excitement!

Yellow. Fast-stepping good times are had with intellectual Yellow.

Orange. Showmen both, Orange and Turquoise share center stage. Powerful opposites balance, each giving substance to the other.

Salmon. An alliance forms with Salmon that sidesteps heavy emotional involvement.

Olive. Light and enjoyable, a barometric Olive/ Turquoise friendship is always understanding.

Brief Affairs

Plum. A friendship with Plum can evolve into a caring, sincere, but sometimes *tense* affair.

Chartreuse. Off to an intense and challenging start, an interlude with Chartreuse moves to romance and/or business.

Yellow. With Yellow exotic fun turns rational, and the affair is over.

Orange. An exciting episode with Orange makes you feel alive. You both give each other a purpose for being.

Salmon. Compatible with Salmon, similar likes draw an affair "at a respectable distance".

Magenta. Fun and flighty, *now-you-see-it-now-you-don't,* Magenta encounters Turquoise. Totally enjoyable!

Blue. A calming, sensitive and loving union with Blue easily moves to loving commitment.

Canteloupe. In search of love and beauty, Canteloupe and Turquoise join in a lovely romance filled with aspiration. It continues!

Purple. Intense and hopeful, Turquoise and Purple dream dreams that come true in lasting romance.

Enduring Romances

Plum. A tense affair with Plum moves into an explosive romance. Caring and sincere, you both learn to depend on each other.

Chartreuse. Intense and challenging moves to meaningful and sincere as your Chartreuse interlude deepens to romance.

Orange. Orange works across the board for you--enduring love, friendship and business partnership.

Salmon. Respecting each other's need for "elbow room", Salmon and Turquoise enjoy a very social, materialistic romance--an enduring commitment without too much soul-searching!

Blue. Blue offers you serenity and peace of mind, while you respect Blue's need to be him or herself.

Canteloupe. From a light aspiring love, a fairy tale romance unfolds with Canteloupe--lovely and lasting!

Purple. Giving each other purpose and meaning, Purple/Turquoise blend in a solid effort to make dreams a reality.

Business Associations

Red. Risk-takers, determined to win, put Red and Turquoise on top of the mark.

Lavender. Lavender/Turquoise allow each other "maneuvering space". Idea people, you both work well in public relations, real estate, fashion and advertising.

Chartreuse. You find Chartreuse a creative, fast-moving business partner.

Orange. Turquoise/Orange work well together. Balancing out each other's weak points, you form a strong force.

Magenta. Very, very flexible, Turquoise and Magenta can adapt to almost any business association.

Beige. Hard-working and fair, a Beige/Turquoise partnership grows to deep trust.

Brown. An intellectual alliance with Brown offers the basis for a stable business partnership.

Salmon. Cutting away emotionalism, Salmon and Turquoise "get down to business".

Indigo. Turquoise and Indigo combine in a goal-oriented association.

Olive. Olive/Turquoise forms a creative, fast-paced partnership.

LAVENDER

Lavender, you attract those seeking love and beauty, and you also draw those who need to protect.

Friendships

Your list of friends, Lavender, is Lengthy!

Magenta. Light-hearted and warm, your friendship with Magenta can have a "touch" of romance.

Purple. A deep sensitive understanding develops with Purple.

Plum. You find a caring and devoted friend in Plum.

Lavender. Whimsical and playful, Lavender may join Lavender in a few romantic and loving daydreams.

Indigo. Understanding friends who appreciate each other "just the way they are", Indigo and Lavender can go across the board--friendship, love and business.

Blue. Spiritual and loving, an enduring friendship with Blue rings in the distinct sound of wedding bells.

Green. Light hearted whimsy and wit can move a Green/Lavender friendship into marriage.

Yellow. Fun and searching, Lavender and Yellow play detective in an intellectual and philosophical friendship. You may even discover a "clue" that leads to an affair.

Canteloupe. An innate understanding with Canteloupe "just is". Happy to be in each other's company, this "smiling" friendship can go across the board.

Salmon. Salmon believes in you, and you believe in Salmon--a mutual admiration society is founded.

Beige. You find a life-long friend in Beige who shares your refined sensibilities.

Olive. In a subtle and stable friendship, you allow Olive to "dream a little"

Turquoise. In a fantastic, three-ring, fast-paced, panoramic circus, a Lavender/Turquoise friendship may find itself joined in a creative business venture.

Brief Affairs

Forever in search of the story book "happy ending", Lavender, you have many affairs.

Magenta. Sensitive, but flighty, a Magenta "mist" quickly evaportates.

Red. Fun and physical, robust Red runs through a Lavender landscape--*briefly!*

Plum. Emotional, kind and sensitive, the affair is fast-paced when Plum puts in an appearance.

Lavender. Lavender meets Lavender for a romantic, evanescent reverie.

Indigo. Deep and emotional, the feelings grow with Indigo.

Blue. Intense, emotional and serious, Blue stays on!

Green. Deep feelings with dreamy yearnings, join Lavender and Green in a fairy tale romance.

Yellow. A light, whirlwind, Yellow affair flies to the clouds and disappears.

Canteloupe. With strong feeling from the start, Lavender and Canteloupe appreciate each other's fantasies. You love to play together, and *you love to play in love* together--and it lasts!

Salmon. Spellbinding Salmon bewitches, but your romantic bubble bursts and the magic melts.

Beige. Lovely and loving, your sophisticated Beige affair with undertones of off-beat excitement continues.

Olive. Secure in the arms of Olive, your spirits soar into enduring romance.

Brown. Rich in dreams, a Brown affair offers a practical foundation for lasting love.

Chartreuse. Intrigued by each other, Chartreuse and Lavender join for a moment of loving warmth.

Orange. You can also savor a brief, dramatic Orange affair!

Enduring Romances

Now for the *happy endings!*

Indigo. Feeling very protective of each other, Lavender and Indigo last in love.

Blue. Blue and you develop a long life of *happy ever after* dreams.

Green. Flights of Lavender/Green fantasy come true as you *make you own fairy tale* a reality.

Canteloupe. An enduring romance with Canteloupe offers nostalgic deep love and understanding.

Beige. Your Beige affair unfolds a romance of strong mutual respect and understanding.

Olive. A good balance is provided here in a romance of dreams and realities, whimsy and solidity.

Brown. Lavender and Brown nurture a solid enduring love.

Business Associations

Lavender, *if you don't have to work, you won't!* But if you do, *you can be very enterprising.*

Turquoise. A Turquoise/Lavender team can keep a whole lot of acts going at the same time. Very socially oriented, you can make good in real estate, public relations, advertising and fashion.

Plum. Lavender/Plum balance in a goal-oriented enterprise.

Indigo. Indigo/Lavender combine in a directed business partnership.

Canteloupe. A Lavender/Canteloupe combo "rake it in" by making *other people's dreams* come true.

Salmon. Creative business minds, Salmon and Lavender also orient themselves to the public.

Olive. Inventive and progressive, Lavender/Olive hold down different ends of the endeavor--Lavender creates, Olive tabulates.

INDIGO

> ***Indigo, you attract powerful colors into your circle.***

Friendships

Choosing to have few friends, Indigo, those you have endure!

Red. Strong and intense, a Red/Indigo friendship has deep emotional ties.

Purple. Driven in search of personal truth, Purple and Indigo unfold a loving spiritual relationship.

Blue. Sensitive and feeling, you and Blue can be more than friends.

Turquoise. As Turquoise and Indigo blend, Indigo stabilizes Turquoise, while Turquoise keeps Indigo stepping lively.

Green. An understanding and hopeful friendship with Green sends out glimmers of lasting romance.

Yellow. Rational and philosophical, Indigo and Yellow share profound intellectual respect.

Beige. Similar material needs and mutual in-depth understanding of life brings Beige and Indigo together.

Olive. Indigo and Olive intensely examine life in solemn philosophical discussions.

Lavender. Understanding friend Lavender likes you just the way you are.

Salmon. Creative and empathetic, a Salmon/Indigo friendship grows.

Brief Affairs

Lavender. Exciting and caring, an affair with Lavender can help you loosen up a little.

Purple. Intense and passionate, your Purple "pause" can perpetuate much continued happiness.

Blue. Highly emotional, intuitive and empathetic, an affair with Blue is brief.

Green. Compassionate, warm and loving, you and Green continue toward lasting romance.

Yellow. An intellectual friendship with Yellow turns to a loving respectful romance.

Beige. Warm, dignified and sincere, your Beige affair is nurtured.

Olive. In need of comfort, you and Olive experience a brief interlude.

Salmon. Compulsive natures make Salmon and Indigo a short-lived romance. Although you might decide to "call it friends".

Canteloupe. Lovely and hopeful, you dream unending dreams with Canteloupe that... quickly end!

Brown. Passionate, loving and volatile, still... romance can continue.

Magenta. Magenta inspires dreams that you balance. This relationship lasts!

Plum. Understanding, rich and warm, Plum and Indigo will blend more than briefly.

Enduring Romances

Your true loves, like your friendships, are lifelong!

Lavender. A strong trusting alliance stems directly from your Lavender love.

Purple. Spiritually intense and physically passionate, You and Purple opt to last.

Green. Understanding and loving, Green/Indigo can blend as one.

Beige. Nurturing each other with admiration and honesty, your affair with Beige blossoms.

Brown. An alliance with Brown becomes a rich, solid, all-for-one, one-for-all loving relationship.

Magenta. Your Magenta dreams wax warm and real, enduring in a lasting love.

Plum. Plum and Indigo continue in romance. Deep and loving dependency develops.

Yellow. Purposeful and strong, Yellow and Indigo remain in love.

Business Associations

A strong, determined and intense planner, business is your "cup of tea"-black, without cream or sugar!

Olive. An Olive/Indigo association can spell out solid scientific business venture.

Red. Red and Indigo overflow... a powerhouse of directed energy!

Purple. A positive goal-oriented team, Purple and Indigo form a strong, powerful alliance.

Turquoise. With emphasis on modern ideas, Turquoise and Indigo combine in a goal-oriented partnership.

Beige. Exciting, rich and substantial, Beige and Indigo find material objectives readily accomplished.

Salmon. Strong and affirmative, Salmon and Indigo can combine in almost any field.

Canteloupe. Warm, industrious and positive in thought, a Canteloupe/Indigo association spells winner!

Chartreuse. A Chartreuse/Indigo team is slated for success.

Plum. Enterprising and constructive, Plum and Indigo are achievers.

Lavender. Lavender/Indigo combine in a creative, innovative, solid enterprise.

Magenta. A partnership of creative consequence, Magenta and Indigo move quickly in an exciting alliance.

SALMON

> ***Salmon, you attract people looking for excitement, people who desire to be social, and people who want to become noteworthy!***

Friendships

Dignitaries and people of high regard can be listed among your friends. Salmon, you like people and can find the best qualities in everyone.

Red. Active, communicative and fun, you join with Red for an exciting social partnership.

Orange. Vital and energetic, an association with Orange is based on similar interests and life-styles.

Lavender. Warm, lively and inspiring, you and Lavender believe in each other.

Indigo. Salmon/Indigo blend as vital, exciting and meaningful friends.

Blue. A trusting relationship blossoms with sincere and caring Blue.

Plum. Strong individuals with similar attitudes, Plum and Salmon quickly become fast friends.

Turquoise. A fast-paced and eccentric association with Turquoise can go across the board--affair, wedding bells and business.

Green. A rational Green "colors" your friendship warm and stimulating.

Brown. Solid, practical, *and* exciting, Brown weighs in well. Friends can become lovers and/or business associates.

Olive. Good friends with exotic tastes, Olive and Salmon might be seen "people watching" at an outdoor cafe "every other Wednesday".

Beige. Sophisticated Beige and Salmon unite to savor the "finer things".

Brief Affairs

Orange. Vital and intense, an Orange/Salmon interlude suggests lasting love.

Lavender. Briefly inspired, you and Lavender experience an emotional episode of intrigue and excitement.

Beige. Your Beige affair, like your friendship, continues to cultivate refined tastes.

Plum. Sensing a familiar tone, Salmon and Plum share the same wave-length. This vibration could last!

Turquoise. A wild, wild affair with Turquoise might bring the unexpected--lasting love!

Green. Caring and substantial, physical and passionate, Green and Salmon pass "go" and move directly to romance.

Brown. Passionate and warm, rich Brown makes a lasting commitment.

Yellow. A material and independent relationship with Yellow shines on.

Canteloupe. A wild affair with Canteloupe is light, fun and brief!

Red. Very communicative, a Red/Salmon involvement moves to lasting love with a lot of chit-chat.

Magenta. A fun affair, Magenta and Salmon, two showpersons very impressed with each other, add color to the social scene.

Indigo. Competitive natures find Salmon and Indigo in a short-lived interlude.

Enduring Romances

Orange. Vital, independent personalities enjoying mutual respect and freedom, Salmon/Orange friends and lovers, move to lasting romance.

Green. Warm friends, caring lovers, Green and Salmon endure with passion, dignity and mutual respect.

Turquoise. Watch out! Sometimes you're a little careless, dear Salmon. Both you and Turquoise have roving eyes. Yet, mutual fascination continues in an exciting, stimulating and enduring relationship.

Brown. Solid friends and passionate lovers, a Brown affair grows into a substantial and strong commitment.

Red. Erratic and fast-paced... forever friends and intense lovers, a strong and caring romance continues for Red and Salmon... *and you both love it!*

Magenta. A fun episode with Magenta turns to devoted romance and endures.

Beige. Deeply felt, your Beige affair continues, strong on caring and commitment.

Plum. Sensuous and warm, Plum and Salmon remain color coordinated, both sharing intense feelings.

Yellow. Material and independent, moves to rational and intellectual as excitement accelerates for Yellow and Salmon.

Business Associations

Fast-stepping and creative, Salmon, no matter what business you start, you "bring home the bacon"!

Indigo. A Salmon/Indigo association is strong and powerful.

Lavender. Lavender/Salmon orient to the public.

Blue. Salmon/Blue combine for a solid enduring business partnership.

Turquoise. Turquoise/Salmon take a "spur of the moment" opportunity and plunge it into a solid business venture.

Green. Spurts of excitement "color" a Green/Salmon combo that is otherwise calm and rational.

Brown. A sturdy association with Brown proves to be good business and investment sense.

Red. Red and Salmon blend for an extremely powerful "won't stop for anything", "never take no for an answer", goal-oriented winning association.

Magenta. A creative partnership, Magenta and Salmon work especially well in the area of sales and communication.

Purple. Intense, Purple/Salmon are innovative.

Orange. A strong-willed team with boundless energy forms as Orange/Salmon unite.

OLIVE

Olive, you attract exotic, dramatic and enterprising people!

Friendships

Olive, you have many, many friends, each and every one of them is very special to you. Your peace-loving nature has chosen them for balance and excitement. In fact, you actually derive your own energy through the entertaining and exotic associations. Indeed, your friends are so entertaining, so amusing and energizing, that you are ready and willing to take the supportive back seat in your relationships. And, tell me, who can resist a ready-made audience?

Brief Affairs

Yellow. Yellow excites you tremendously. You "head" for a very rational, conceptually oriented affair that pays extra dividends in romance and/or business.

Lavender. Inspired by vaporous Lavender, your supportive nature balances a wonderful combination that easily grows to enduring love.

Indigo. Attracted by mutual innermost thoughts, Indigo and Olive are drawn together for a brief affair that can easily turn into a business association if you are both so inclined.

Red. Vital, enthusiastic and passionate, Red sweeps in and, very possibly, stays. With Red taking the lead, you can both move to business or lasting love .

Plum. An affair with Plum will be sensuous and understanding. It ripens to a *plum-p* and juicy romance!

Green. Friendly, easy-going and mellow, Green and Olive have much to share--affair, enduring love and, perhaps, a business venture.

Brown. Solid and stable, Olive and Brown are alike in many ways. Rich in mutual interests, lasting love can easily color your future.

Orange. Orange will certainly heat up your affair. From a rational and compatible friendship, feelings grow into deep respect for each other's well-being.

Canteloupe. Fascinated by the freedom Canteloupe offers, your stability balances this vibrant melon.

Blue. A Blue affair is low-keyed, but solid. You succumb to enduring romance.

Enduring Romances

Yellow. Offering solidity and respectability to Yellow, a balance for lasting love is struck. Your fascination and excitement flourish.

Lavender. Lavender enjoys your stabilizing influence. You continue romantically inspired.

Red. Red's fast-paced innovative force keeps you hopping, and you relish it! Love deepens.

Plum. From sensuous and understanding, to rich and trusting, Plum and Olive endure.

Green. A friendly, easy-going and mellow Green affair intensifies. You are both totally honest and sincere.

Brown. Rich in creative thought and mutual affection, Brown blossoms, as do you.

Blue. Interdependence grows as a Blue/Olive love unfolds a solid commitment.

Orange. A deep understanding with Orange builds. This could be it!

Canteloupe. ...and so could Canteloupe, you lucky Olive, you!

Business Associations

Stabilizing in love, you are solid in business.

Yellow. Business with Yellow is practical and rational.

Lavender. Lavender/Olive work best in a light venture, such as a shop or store.

Indigo. Solid, durable and intense, Indigo means business. Very serious and very directed in your associations, you will profit together.

Red. In a balanced working relationship, Red innovates, as Olive and Red combine to construct "realities".

Plum. Keep the operation simple and Olive/Plum "rake it in"! You are both hard-working, trusting and trustworthy.

Green. Much in common in love and business, Green means "go" in love, and "green" in business.

Brown. Rich creative thoughts combine in a diligent, hard-working Brown/Olive partnership.

Orange. A vital, strong business force becomes a reality with Olive/Orange in the picture.

Purple. Both workers, Purple/Olive balance well. Purple seeks out new ventures and Olive supports whatever seems solid.

Turquoise. Fast-moving, your association with Turquoise will be very creative.

Chartreuse. A Chartreuse/Olive team is modern, creative and very able to deal with reality.

Blue. Practical Olive/Blue combine for a solid goal-oriented association.

MAGENTA

Magenta, you are highly magnetic and very well liked. Everyone is drawn to you!

Friendships

Heavy friendships are burdensome to your dreamy nature!

Red. *Red*-ily gravitating to whimsy, Red supplies lots of surprises--one of them being a whirlwind affair!

Magenta. Without a doubt, spontaneous Magenta and Magenta strike up a carefree alliance.

Lavender. Light and lively, your friendship with Lavender will be filled with entertaining daydreams.

Blue. On the other hand, Blue offers deep friendship and understanding. Mutually sympathetic, here's a solid shot at wedding bells.

Green. A well-balanced, kind and giving friendship develops with Green.

Olive. Olive offers a secure base for Magenta's "travels", while Magenta whimsy entertains Olive.

Canteloupe. A very social friendship with Canteloupe can find the fun and excitement continuing in a lasting romance.

Brief Affairs

Green. Now, here's a switch! Kind and giving, your affair with Green turns to lasting friendship.

Blue. Comforting and feeling, a Blue/Magenta affair gives great odds at lasting love.

Red. Brief and passionate Red whirls Magenta through a memorable episode.

Purple. A romance with Purple will not be brief. There's a good balance here.

Lavender. Dreamy and romantic, an interlude with Lavender blossoms into another lovely friendship.

Orange. Carefree and barometric, an Orange affair takes you to the skies and back again. Still, a very good possibility for continuing romance.

Turquoise. A quick-silver tempting Turquoise tryst may be over before you realize it's begun.

Beige. Comfortable and easy, a friendly affair with Beige easily unfolds enduring love and/or a business ally.

Canteloupe. Gentle and generous, this affair nurtures mutual interdependence and a very good bet for lasting romance!

Salmon. No doubt about it, Salmon and Magenta will give it a go. Both love to astound. Mutual respect grows into business and/or romance.

Indigo. Magenta inspires solid Indigo to dream a little--very real and warm love endures.

Chartreuse. With Chartreuse it stays light!

Enduring Romances

Blue. Deep understanding, harmony and balance is struck with Blue. Blue understands Magenta, while Magenta finds strength in Blue.

Purple. A very comfortable balance, Purple offers positive direction and identity, while Magenta "lightens up" Purple with whimsy and positive feedback.

Salmon. Mutual respect moves Salmon and Magenta into the winner's circle--both showpeople, social and exciting, love continues to grow.

Beige. Magenta and Beige "wear" very well. That friendly affair develops into lasting romance and/or a business venture.

Orange. Excited, energetic and interested in many things, Orange and Magenta continue their "barometric bounce" into lasting love.

Canteloupe. Gentle and loving, Canteloupe and Magenta unfold mutual trust and confidence.

Indigo. Balanced by solid Indigo, Magenta adds a little frivolity into a loving, lasting romance.

Business Associations

Steadily channelled in one direction, your highly creative energy spells s-u-c-c-e-s-s!

Salmon. Both social "lights", Magenta/Salmon showmanship teams for an innovative business with Salmon definitely holding down the practical end!

Indigo. A creative Magenta/Indigo partnership makes substantial business sense.

Turquoise. An exciting "visionary" association blossoms as Magenta/Turquoise blend.

Brown. A great business balance--Brown handles the tedium you hate, as you pursue your innovative interests.

Beige. Magenta and Beige offer a sturdy and creative working balance.

Canteloupe. In a business that deals directly with the public, a Canteloupe/Magenta alliance proves positive, enthusiastic and profitable.

PLUM

Plum, you attract those looking for a strong sensitive person, and many who strive for success are drawn to your magnetism.

Friendships

A warm and caring friend who is basically out for the other guy, *"Trust"* is the banner you carry. A snob at a distance who can, many times, be heard saying, "Oh, I just can't believe it! How could anyone do such a thing?" You are exactly the opposite in your personal relationships. "In the clinches" you compassionately and sympathetically understand how "things *can* happen". While *appearing* aloof, deep down you are a honey bun!

Adaptable without fear of compromising your own identity, you can befriend any color. But, friends beware! *Plum can walk away from any commitment not found to be worthy of trust and loyalty!*

Brief Affairs and Enduring Romances

Plum, you are very selective in your love, but so innately warm and protective, and adaptable to those you cherish that you could, very possibly, have a brief affair with any color. And an affair would be very brief, indeed, if your lover's trustworthiness or loyalty was questioned.

You excel, however, in enduring romances. Never threatened by the ones you love, you easily mold yourself through your concern for and devotion to the subjects of your affection. Readily adapting without losing your individuality, this rare quality allows you to enjoy an enduring love with any color personality.

Strong-willed, you are capable in any situation. Emotional and passionate, you are forever practical. Family-oriented, you are empathetic without being condescending. So, pick your color-mate, you have *carte blanche.*

Business Associations

Plum, you are good in sales and dealing with the public. Communications, TV, public relations and design are also good possibilities.

Indigo. Business with Indigo will be creative, practical and enduring.

Lavender. A light easy venture with Lavender might find you partners in a card shop.

Beige. A sophisticated svelte operation with Beige might mean TV, public relations, documentaries or communications in general.

Orange. A Plum/Orange combo will do well in any business as long as it is exciting and continually presents new challenges.

Olive. A hard-working, trusting association is enjoyed with Olive. It's best to keep the operation simple.

Brown. A solid and rich partnership with Brown might mean a career in investments, but you are both so adaptable that almost anything works.

Plum. Plum and Plum merge in an intense, vital and creative alliance.

Purple. With Purple, a good work force solidifies. Together you can make a whole lot happen!

BROWN

Substantial, Brown, *you attract practical people, people who need someone to "lean on" and you are very attractive to employers.*

Friendships

Yellow. A Yellow/Brown Friendship will be good-natured and practical.

Orange. Orange and Brown blend in a warm, substantial and kind friendship.

Purple. A spiritual and materialistic balance is struck in a Brown/Purple alliance.

Plum. Exciting and active, you and your Plum pal are continually "thinking and doing".

Chartreuse. Intellectually disposed, you and Chartreuse hone each other mentally.

Green. A warm, gentle and trusting friendship with Green can move to true love.

Beige. You wax eloquent with Beige. Both very verbal, you share refined sensibilities.

Salmon. A quick stepping, exciting, creative, materialistically oriented friendship is enjoyed with Salmon.

Olive. Uncomplicated and easy, you and your Olive chum champion causes and join clubs together.

Brief Affairs

Brown, you are really not all that good at brief affairs. Although, a momentary "indulgence" is not out of the question. When deeply aroused, you almost always follow through to lasting romance.

Red, however, might seduce you into a wildly intense and passionate affair. You are so excited and awed by the carefree sense of freedom that Red exudes, that you just can't help yourself. The affair will be well worth it-and not all that brief!

Enduring Romances

Purple. From an emotional and passionate start, your Purple love endures, solid and intense.

Plum. Traditional in thought, your Plum romance continues with warmth.

Green. Compassionate companions, Brown/Green blend in interdependence. A caring, kind, trusting and stable relationship evolves.

Salmon. Passionate, uncomplicated and wild at the start, your Salmon romance turns to solid, substantial commitment.

Beige. From an intense beginning, you and Beige remain directed and positive in your love.

Olive. A loving, practical affair with Olive deepens as you both seek to fulfill each other's needs and happiness.

Indigo. An intense wild affair with Indigo continues. Romance is passionate and emotional ties bind.

Lavender. What seemed to be whimsical, your Lavender affair endures in mutual appreciation and a warm loving romance. You feel protective.

Business Associations

When needed, Brown, you can mold yourself and channel your energies to accommodate any practical and workable venture. You can work with almost anyone. Sizing up a situation, you *"make it work"* for you. Very pragmatic, you can stand behind the scenes with full appreciation and recognition of your own value. What's more, you will not allow business to affect you emotionally.

MAGNETIC ATTRACTIONS IN BRIEF

	Friendships	Affairs	Romances	Business
Yellow	Lavender	Lavender		
	Indigo	Indigo	Indigo	
	Blue	Blue		Blue
	Turquoise	Turquoise		
	Green	Green	Green	Green
	Chartreuse	Chartreuse	Chartreuse	Chartreuse
	Red	Red	Red	Red
	Yellow	Yellow	Yellow	
	Purple			
	Canteloupe	Canteloupe	Canteloupe	
	Orange	Orange	Orange	Orange
	Brown			Brown
		Olive	Olive	Olive
		Salmon	Salmon	
Red	Blue	All Colors	Blue	Blue
	Yellow		Yellow	Yellow
	Red		Red	Red
	Beige		Beige	Beige

	Magenta			
	Chartreuse			
	Indigo			Indigo
	Turquoise			Turquoise
	Canteloupe			
	Salmon		Salmon	Salmon
	Purple		Purple	Purple
			Olive	Olive
			Brown	Brown
			Orange	Orange
			Plum	
Blue	All Colors	Red	Red	Red
		Blue	Blue	Blue
		Yellow		Yellow
		Magenta	Magenta	
		Purple	Purple	Purple
		Lavender	Lavender	
		Indigo		
		Turquoise	Turquoise	
		Green	Green	Green
		Canteloupe	Canteloupe	Canteloupe
		Olive	Olive	Olive
		Plum	Plum	
		Chartreuse	Chartreuse	
		Beige	Beige	
				Salmon

	Freindships	Affairs	Romances	Business
Orange	Turquiose	Turquoise	Turquoise	Turquoise
	Purple	Purple	Purple	Purple
	Plum			Plum
	Yellow	Yellow	Yellow	Yellow
	Canteloupe	Canteloupe	Canteloupe	Canteloupe
	Orange	Orange	Orange	Orange
	Salmon	Salmon	Salmon	Salmon
	Brown			Brown
	Olive	Olive	Olive	Olive
	Chartreuse	Chartreuse		Chartreuse
		Green	Green	Green
		Red	Red	Red
				Beige
		Magenta	Magenta	
		Lavender		
Green	All Colors	Magenta		
		Plum		
		Salmon	Salmon	Salmon
			Yellow	Yellow
			Canteloupe	Canteloupe
			Orange	Orange

			Blue	Blue
			Olive	Olive
			Brown	Brown
			Lavender	
			Indigo	
Purple	Green			
	Red	Red	Red	Red
	Blue	Blue	Blue	Blue
	Yellow			
	Orange	Orange	Orange	Orange
	Brown	Brown	Brown	Brown
	Purple	Purple	Purple	
	Indigo	Indigo	Indigo	Indigo
	Lavender			
		Turquoise	Turquoise	
		Chartreuse	Chartreuse	Chartreuse
		Magenta	Magenta	
		Plum	Plum	Plum
				Beige
				Salmon
				Olive

	Friendships	Affairs	Romance	Business
Canteloupe	Red			
	Lavender	Lavender	Lavender	Lavender
	Magenta	Magenta	Magenta	Magenta
	Orange	Orange	Orange	Orange
	Plum	Plum	Plum	
	Chartreuse	Chartreuse	Chartreuse	Chartreuse
	Blue	Blue	Blue	Blue
	Canteloupe	Canteloupe		Canteloupe
	Yellow	Yellow	Yellow	Yellow
		Turquoise	Turquoise	
		Indigo		Indigo
		Green	Green	Green
		Salmon		
		Beige	Beige	Beige
				Brown
Beige	Brown		Brown	All Colors
	Chartreuse		Chartreuse	
	Lavender		Lavender	
	Red		Red	
	Plum		Plum	
	Indigo		Indigo	
	Beige		Beige	

	Olive			
	Salmon		Salmon	
		Canteloupe	Canteloupe	
		Turquoise		
			Magenta	
			Blue	
Chartreuse	Red	Red		
	Chartreuse	Chartreuse	Chartreuse	Chartreuse
	Yellow	Yellow	Yellow	Yellow
	Canteloupe	Canteloupe	Canteloupe	Canteloupe
	Orange	Orange		Orange
	Brown			Brown
	Olive			Olive
	Beige	Beige	Beige	Beige
	Turquoise	Turquoise	Turquoise	Turquoise
				Indigo
		Purple	Purple	Purple
	Plum	Plum	Plum	
		Lavender		
		Blue	Blue	
		Magenta		

	Friendships	Affairs	Romances	Business
Turquoise	Red			Red
	Plum	Plum	Plum	
	Lavender			Lavender
	Indigo			Indigo
	Green			
	Chartreuse	Chartreuse	Chartreuse	Chartreuse
	Yellow	Yellow		
	Orange	Orange		Orange
	Salmon	Salmon	Orange	Salmon
	Olive		Salmon	Olive
		Magenta		Magenta
		Blue	Blue	
		Canteloupe	Canteloupe	
				Beige
		Purple	Purple	
				Brown
Lavender	Magenta	Magenta		
		Red		
	Purple	Purple		
	Plum	Plum		Plum
	Lavender	Lavender		
	Indigo	Indigo	Indigo	Indigo

	Blue	Blue	Blue	
	Green	Green	Green	
	Yellow	Yellow		
	Canteloupe	Canteloupe	Canteloupe	Canteloupe
	Salmon	Salmon		Salmon
	Beige	Beige	Beige	
	Olive	Olive	Olive	Olive
		Brown	Brown	
	Turquoise			Turquoise
		Chartreuse		
		Orange		
	Red			Red
Indigo	Purple	Purple	Purple	Purple
	Blue	Blue		
	Turquoise			Turquoise
	Green	Green	Green	
	Yellow	Yellow	Yellow	
	Beige	Beige	Beige	Beige
	Olive	Olive		Olive
	Salmon	Salmon		Salmon
		Canteloupe		Canteloupe
		Brown	Brown	
		Magenta	Magenta	Magenta
		Plum	Plum	Plum
	Lavender	Lavender	Lavender	Lavender
				Chartreuse

	Freindships	Affairs	Romances	Business
Salmon	Orange	Orange	Orange	Orange
	Lavender	Lavender		Lavender
	Indigo			Indigo
	Blue			Blue
	Plum	Plum	Plum	
	Turquoise	Turquoise	Turquoise	Turquoise
	Green	Green	Green	Green
	Brown	Brown	Brown	Brown
	Beige	Beige	Beige	
	Olive			
		Yellow	Yellow	
		Canteloupe		
	Red	Red	Red	Red
		Magenta	Magenta	Magenta
				Purple
Olive	All Colors	Yellow	Yellow	Yellow
		Lavender	Lavender	Lavender
		Indigo		Indigo
		Red	Red	Red
		Plum	Plum	Plum
		Green	Green	Green
		Brown	Brown	Brown

		Orange	Orange	Orange
		Canteloupe	Canteloupe	
				Purple
				Turquoise
				Chartreuse
		Blue	Blue	Blue
Magenta	Red	Red		
	Magenta			
	Lavender	Lavender		
	Blue	Blue	Blue	
	Green	Green		
	Olive			
	Canteloupe	Canteloupe	Canteloupe	Canteloupe
		Purple	Purple	
		Orange	Orange	
		Turquoise		Turquoise
		Beige	Beige	Beige
		Salmon	Salmon	Salmon
		Indigo	Indigo	Indigo
		Chartreuse		
				Brown

	Friendships	Affairs	Romances	Business
Plum	All Colors	All Colors	All Colors	Indigo
				Lavender
				Beige
				Orange
				Olive
				Brown
				Plum
				Purple
Brown	Yellow			All Colors
	Orange			
	Purple		Purple	
	Plum		Plum	
	Chartreuse			
	Green		Green	
	Beige		Beige	
	Salmon		Salmon	
	Olive		Olive	
		Red		
			Indigo	
			Lavender	

CREATING WITH COLOR

Are you beginning to notice how you, personally, gravitate to particular color energies? How on some days you can't get enough of a certain tone while, other days, "a little dab'll do ya"? Are you beginning to understand why some friendships are so color-fast they just don't fade no matter how many dunkings you take or how many times you are hung out to dry... or have nature's mating magnets more than monkeyed with your emotions? (Considered giving your dates the color test?) Then again, perhaps, you are getting the idea that, maybe, you can't quite *see eye-to-eye* with so-and-so because you are each confined to your own colored *prisms.*

When you crave energy and need to be social, have you found yourself ogling Undulating **Oranges?** Are Raucous **Reds** repulsive when you're emotionally exterminated? When you've got the "Blues", no doubt about it, sympathetic **Blues** offer comfort and caring.

Need a dream? Dial **L-A-V-E-N-D-E-R!** Short on fresh ideas? A well-spring of solarization, **Chartreuse** will radiate the rescue! Burnt out in business, just thank your *lucky colors* for **Brown!**

You may have begun to wonder just how far this color business can go. Well, my "aura-cle", there is much you can accomplish with your new found knowledge.

Earlier, I said you were an artist, *as well as* a magnetic energy painting whirring your multi-toned rainbow through time and space. With your newly found palette you can now deliberately begin to add color and tones that can reinforce your Basic Energy, modify a mood, balance a Blend, a Flash or your very foundation. You can make changes in your relationships, your environment and your life.

You can "paint" your aspirations into reality, buffer with neutrals, "draw" in your fondest dreams with magnetic color, refine your vibration, signal, protect and be comforted by color.

If you have been wondering whether or not your Basic Colorscope can change, the answer is yes, but not easily. This can occur *only if your **Basic Energy Pattern** modifies (It can mutate over a period of time, or be modified by a very dramatic upheaval in your ideas, your physicality and/or your emotions).* In general, it is very likely that the configurations you now have will **remain constant** for most, if not for all, of your adult life.

Similar to a *Stellar and Planetary horoscope,* you now have your basic "chart". What you do with your total range or "scope" is up to you. In this section we will introduce you to the possibilities.

BALANCING (YOUR) VIBRATIONS

Are you a Lavender Lost?
Too Intensely Indigo?
A Careless Canteloupe?
A Bogged-down Blue?
A Boring Blasé Beige?
A Greedy Gone Amuck Green?
A Dishevelled Chartreuse?
A Ride-over Rough-shod Red?
A Power Hungry Purple?
An Overly Awesome Orange?
A Pompous Plum? An Irate Yowling Yellow?
A Tumbled Turquoise? A Sanctimonious Salmon?
A Much Too Momentary Magenta?
A Bureaucratic Brown Bear?
An Ole "Stick in the Mud" Olive?

Of course you're not, but I'll bet you know someone who is!

Indeed, many Blends and Flashes offer the opportunity to counterbalance an individual Colorscope configuration. But still, we can all get bogged down from time to time, and now and again are caught off guard by life's bumps and burrs and our own trips to fantasy land.

The right color, however, can help counter a power outage, short circuit, flicker or overload. Functioning as a physical, mental, emotional and/or spiritual stabilizer, a little color can balance you right back into the ball game.

So, if you, or someone you know, needs a little color compensation, subtle or intense, the right adaptor can steady the boat.

Color balancers present themselves in any number of forms, shapes and sizes--from a basket of flowers sent to a slightly off-the-beat friend, to a scarf, a sweater, a colorful stone or a new car. It's the color that's important. In-house color compensators might include strategically placed color accents--a vase, a throw pillow, a knick-knack, table cloth or even a new coat of paint.... And, for personal use, anything from a piece of jewelry to an inexpensive fabric swatch or that paint sample will work--something that can be referred to throughout the day.

And, to add more punch to your purpose, when you focus on your selected sash or favored fedora, deeply "inhale" your balance color. "Pulling" the color into your aura, "see" the color become part of your whirring magnetic force field .

Color Balancers

Colors that compensate, adjust and rebalance your Basic Energy vibration include:

Red can balance a bout of depression, especially if it is associated with physical weakness.

Bright sunny **Yellow**, warms to balance sadness. *(Hmm... to send red or yellow roses, what a lovely dilemma.)*

To counter confusion, worry and restlessness try a little **Blue**. *(A day in, or near, deep blue waters under a blue, blue sky banishes a heck of a lot!)*

Orange compensates feelings of failure and low self-esteem, eradicates irrationalism and counters a sense of loneliness and solitude. *(A bowl of oranges on the table can be a very practical solution.)*

To tune your energy to the Earth and Humanity call in **Green**. *(Tune into your house plant, take a walk in the garden.)*

To counter confusion boredom and inertia try **Chartreuse**, *(Slice open a lime, wear a vibrant peridot....)*

"Loosening up" the energy vibration, **Magenta** offers a flight of fancy and a stepping stone to Spiritual commitment. *(Clothing, tableware, flowers, a color swatch for meditation--all work very well.)*

Seeking purpose and direction in life? **Purple** balances Spiritual Blue with Red-reality, while **Magenta's** "creative Red-Purple space" softens the search. *(Colored swatches are ready access--plush velvet, or an amethyst, can add comfort to the quest.)*

Amplifying self-love, **Canteloupe** counters a "lack of self worth". This lovely melon will also stimulate an appreciation for creativity. *(As close as your fruit bowl, or a silk blouse or shirt can stimulate appreciation.)*

An emotional energy endurance compensator, **Beige** allows you to remain unaffected by a "rival", so that you can continue to work on. *(Natural undyed fibers, champagne and bone-colored clothing are good bets.)*

Turquoise clarifies. Used to open new "avenues", It seeks the truth. *(The fabulous turquoise waters in the Bahamas are great "avenues", but colored beads or a slice of the magical stone can be easily carried.)*

Balancing misinterpretation and a lack of concentration, **Indigo** helps gain insight and mental penetration. The blend of Blue/Purple signifies Practicality moving toward Intuition. *(Staring into the deep blue-purple heavens on an almost starless night helps to focus.)*

Lavender soothes, tranquillizes, and refines spirituality. *(Definitely lavender roses for me.)*

Olive balances out unrealistic and negative thought. *(Consider olive drab army fatigues--very grounding.)*

Want to bring someone out of hiding? **Salmon's** subtle balance helps functioning at a human level, *(A tin of salmon at the deli, a few sliced onions and I'm functioning--just kidding.)*

Engendering a feeling of well-being, **Plum** counters depression. *(A bowl of plums on the counter, or an outfit in the lush brown-red-purple offers the comfort of rich, creative substantiality.)*

Brown grounds you in Physicality, balances light-headedness and flightiness. It is a great equalizer for the Purples. *(How about the grounding color in a "chocolate bar", rich brown suedes, the trunk of an ancient tree!)*

Neutral Balancers

Compensating the emotions, **Gray** calms and subdues. *(Ever travel through a mist in the car or hypnotically stare into the fog?)*

Black and **White** function differently from the other tones and hues. B*alancing with comfort as you undergo transition*, they absorb and reflect, rather than *alter,* a basic energy pattern. **White** "amplifies" your basic energy *like the radiating sunlight,* while **Black** "absorbs and soothes" *like the deep, dark night.* Both can be worn by any Color Personality without affecting change.

So, for a Lavender Lost, you might consider a grounding pair of Orange boots or an Olive scarf!

Too Intensely Indigo, could lighten up with a little Magenta, Turquoise, and/or Yellow.

A Careless Canteloupe might tighten up with a dash of Green or Olive, some Grounding Brown or Red.

Bogged-down Blue could do with a little refreshing Chartreuse, elevating Purple, dreamy Lavender and Magenta magic.

Boring Blasé Beige can call on Chartreuse, Orange, Red, Salmon and Turquoise.

A Greedy Gone Amuck Green could do with Blue, Red, some "giving" Canteloupe "to open up", and warming Yellow.

A Dishevelled Chartreuse could balance with Indigo or Blue, Yellow, and Lavender's Orange boots.

To slow down ***A Ride-over Rough-shod Red,*** balance with sensitizing Blue, spiritual Indigo, powerful Purple, respectful Beige, Turquoise and/or calming Gray.

A Power-Hungry Purple might ease up with spiritual Lavender, "giving" Canteloupe, or balance with Green.

An Overly Awesome Orange could subdue with a Beaker of Blue and a shot of Olive, Indigo or Green.

A Pompous Plum, would respond to Blue, Green, Canteloupe, Salmon, Lavender and Indigo.

An Irate Yowling Yellow needs Blue and Lavender, some dignified Gray and inky Indigo.

A Tumbled Turquoise can focus with Chartreuse, Green and Yellow, and ground with Brown.

A Sanctimonious Salmon could use sympathetic Blue, or Beige, "open up" Turquoise, tolerant Olive and accepting Green.

To help stabilize ***A Much Too Momentary Magenta,*** try some grounding Brown, stable Olive, Indigo, Plum and Earth-balance Green.

That Bureaucratic Brown Bear could use some harmonizing Green, or sympathetic Blue, "open and giving" Canteloupe, refreshing Chartreuse, stimulating Red or Orange.

Ole Stick in the Mud Olive could dive into Chartreuse, Turquoise, Canteloupe, Magenta and Salmon.

Are you getting the idea? Whatever the imbalance, look for colors that gently counter.

ASPIRING COLORS
(And Neutrals)

Are you a Blue whose significant other wishes you were more Earthy?

Would you, personally, like to become more Powerful?

Spiritual?

Refined?

Intellectual?

Intense?

Organized?

More Relaxed around people?

More Rational?

More Distinguished?

Materially Comfortable?

More in Harmony with the World?

Do you need to hold it together before a big "move" or power play?

Power Color can do it!

Here's How!

Ambitious for ***Power?*** Wear Red!
Want to be more ***Dynamic?***
Stoke your Earthly fires with RED!
Breathe Red! Think Red! Eat Red!

To couch before ***a "Power Move",***
to Calm, to Look Distinguished?
Move into the mist with GRAY!

Looking for **Change?**
TURQUOISE tempts transition!

Seeking ***Spiritual Ideals?***
Then LAVENDER appeals!
Or, is it ***Spiritual Peace that you pursue?***
If this is true, then BLUE is your hue!

Intrigued by the Unseen and ***Intuition?***
Life need more Definition?
Want to be more "in the know"?
INDIGO's the way to go!

Looking toward more ***Energy?***
Try a surge of SALMON!

Seeking ***Higher Knowledge?***
YELLOW gives the mental edge!

Struggling for ***Strength of Purpose?***
POWER PURPLE is where the worth is!

Longing to be ***Gentle, but Strong?***
Sensitize with CANTELOUPE.

Need some ***Hope and a few Dreams?***
Rent-a-MAGENTA!

Aspire to ***Physical Strength, Happiness and Social Skill?***
TONES OF ORANGE fill the bill.

Looking for Truth?
Travel on TURQUOISE! It opens doors.

Aspire to ***Actively Search, Absorb and Amplify?***
Cloak in BLACK!

Need to ***Magnetically Pull, Reflect and Amplify?***
Wish, will and wear WHITE!

Looking to ***Freshen Mental Juices?***
Go for LIMES and CHARTREUSES!

Seeking ***Earthly Richness and Comfort?***
Keep BROWN around!

Aspire to a ***Happy, Warm, Fulfilling Life?***
PLUM helps to buffer strife!

Looking to be more ***Reasonable and Rational?***
OLIVE is the key!

Desire to be more ***Dominant and Enjoy the Gusto?***
Call for SALMON!

Aspire to ***Material Refinements?***
Go BONE to BEIGE!

Wish you could ***Relate better Physically and Materially?***
BROWN is sound!

Aspire to be a ***Clear Crisp Thinker?***
Need your thoughts refreshed?
Boost with CHARTREUSE!

Looking for ***Peace, Harmony, and***
Subtle Strength in life Through Giving?
GREEN is serene!

If you aspire to any of the preceding,
employ the corresponding colors.
They are Power!

REFINING YOUR VIBRATION

Fine tuning with Power Color

Now that you can sweep swirls of color through your aura to balance, and wave your energy wand to draw your dreams, aspirations and ambitions into your future, The subtle aspects of Power Color can also help you to fine tune your Colorscope.

Colors for Refinement

Red. Particularly good if you are low-keyed and you want to become noticed, Red will help you to think more positively, direct your energy more positively and become more aggressive. Red will help you make a clear statement of your purpose.

Yellow will tune you to conceptual and intellectual understanding.

Blue calms, allowing you to reach out and fine tune your spiritual needs, whatever they may be.

Orange offers pride, ambition, energy, practicality, warmth, understanding, and empathy.

Green refines your vibration in order to move with the forces of nature, tune into the world and the people around you.

Purple refines and stimulates creative impulses and creative clarity.

Canteloupe sensitizes to beauty in all forms. It brings money, gives youth and teaches how to give.

Beige helps to gain and refine your inner strength. It helps you to forget yourself, and to "handle yourself" without letting "personal things" get in the way.

Chartreuse refines your mental electricity. If you are bogged down, your mind is cleared and stimulated.

Turquoise opens up thought, makes you more expansive, invites change, new thoughts, ideas and perspectives.

Lavender refines your search for goodness, spirituality and kindness.

Indigo refines your depth of understanding, giving a deeper comprehension of universal concepts.

Salmon refines your communication skills, helps you to become more alert, energetic and sensitive. It allows you to become more personable and powerful without being overbearing.

Olive refines your practical nature, helps you to plan for the future and helps your endurance.

Magenta lightens your surrounding pressures. It frees your spirit and gives you the "freedom to breathe".

Plum helps you to be social while working on a spiritual level. It hones the attribute of kindness.

Brown refines your endurance and substance inviting a life that is physically and materially rich and meaningful.

Refining Neutrals

Gray refines your strength in neutrality.

White fine tunes your own basic energy.

Black. For adventure, fine tune with Black.

Energy-colors can be "painted" into your magnetic field in many ways. You can wear them, eat them, drink them, look at them, inhale them, place accents or whole areas of color where you live and/or work. You can mentally motivate energy color into your magnetic force field by visualizing their presence. And, if you cannot actually see color, think of something that you associate with the energy.

To give an example--You are in class and the professor is lecturing about something that seems way over your head. You look around the assembly, find someone wearing yellow and tune in. Or, feel the energy of the sun flooding into your aura.

Later that day, you see someone to whom you are very attracted and you definitely want to be noticed, but you are in a crowd wearing misty gray. Mentally make your outfit bright Orange by tuning into an orange scarf someone is wearing, or surround yourself with the energy of the ripe glowing fruit, or a screaming Red fire engine. *(It depends on how you want to become noticed, ablaze or aglow!)*

Comes mid-afternoon, and with it, an energy letdown. *Paint* in some Salmon, a Red/Orange Blend, maybe some snappy electrical Chartreuse with the jolt of a lime-ade without sugar to refresh your mental waters.

Another example--Lately, life has been oppressive. You are having trouble sleeping. When you awaken, you feel trapped in your situation and there is no end in sight. You call in, visualize, and begin to breath in Magenta, while you place touches of Turquoise around the apartment. Magenta offers you the opportunity to "dream" and Turquoise works to open up "change".

It's sort of like playing with the color adjustment knobs on the TV set-a little more Green here, Red there.... It keeps the picture clear, color balanced and in focus. It's also fun. And incredibly, it works!

Whatever the situation,
Power Color Can help!

COMFORT COLORS

Another interesting and very helpful aspect is the way in which Power Colors offer comfort. They can give comfort in protection to offering comfort in comfort itself.

Red comforts with Power!

Yellow comforts with Positive Thought.

Blue comforts with Serenity.

Orange comforts with Comfort.

Green offers comfort in giving and fruitfulness.

Purple comforts with Protection.

Canteloupe offers comfort in Soft Warmth, the feeling of Youth, Freedom and Grace, Free Thinking, and comforts with Inspiration to Wealth and Beauty.

Beige offers Inner Strength, Pride, and Self-appreciation.

Chartreuse comforts with the Modern and New--things that make you feel alive!

Turquoise comforts by allowing you to "Open Yourself Up" to new avenues of thought.

Lavender comforts with Romance, Self-kindness, and warm, soft, Gentle Surroundings.

Indigo offers comfort in Deep Spiritual Rest.

Salmon comforts with Energy, Pride and Alertness.

Olive comforts with Feelings of Solidity and Endurance and with the comfort of Blending in with the crowd.

Magenta comforts with Dreams and Hopes.

Plum comforts with Feelings of full, solid, Creative Warmth and Richness.

Brown allows you to Blend In.

Comfort Neutrals

Gray comforts via Protection by way of Untouchable Neutrality,

White offers Protection through Reflection.

Black can Protect by Repulsion, and comfort through the Amplification of your Feelings..

WEARING COLOR

Have you ever wondered why Buddhist monks wear yellow?

Why Black and White are colors of mourning?

Why Red and White are marriage colors?

Why the Virgin Mary is dressed in Blue?

The Reasons for wearing Power Colors (and Power Neutrals) are revealed below. Knowing how and when to use them without a doubt spells P-O-W-E-R!

Power Colors

Red

When you want to show Strength, *Counter* physical weakness, emotional weakness, mental weakness wear Red. If your ambition is power, if you want to become more dynamic wear Red. For Comfort in Power wear Red. To counter depression wear Red. To emphasize that you are, indeed, powerful, wear Red!

Yellow

If you want to attract intellectual, fun-loving, ambitious people wear Yellow. To be noticed, to amplify Positive Thought wear Yellow. If you need an aid in your aspirations to Higher Knowledge, wear Yellow. If you want to feel happy and search in an overt manner, wear Yellow!

Blue

For peace, endurance and consistency, and to help you in your Spiritual aspirations, wear Blue.

Orange

To be more assertive, outgoing, warm, self-secure, strong and social wear Orange. To be happy, to balance a feeling of failure and loneliness wear Orange. To attract organizers, leaders, comfort lovers and ambitious people wear Orange. To attract a social crowd or person wear Orange.

Green

Looking for peace, harmony and unity? Wear Green. Want to attract someone looking for the same? Wear Green. Are you looking for subtle strength through a life of giving? Wear Green. It should be noted that the reasons for wearing Green change by the intensity of the color you wear and your mental attitude.

Purple

Traditionally a "royal" and "artist's color", Purple is worn as a shield for protection. It is worn to be in control of others, to develop a strength of purpose, and worn to counter self-fears. It is worn to stimulate self-creativity and creative direction.

Canteloupe

Canteloupe is worn to attract youth, money and to display beauty. It is worn to become more sensitive and gentle without compromising strength. If you want to feel more youthful, soft, warm, hopeful, giving and alive wear Canteloupe. If you need to love yourself more and appreciate your self more, wear Canteloupe. If you want to hone your appreciation for beauty, right! It's Canteloupe.

Beige

Need to stay neutral, balance your emotions, be conservative and respectful? Wear Beige. Looking to attract refinement, bright people who make a solid physical stand? Wear Beige--*especially if you aspire to future assets!*

Chartreuse

Want to feel alive, electric and directed? Wear Chartreuse! Trying to attract clear *avant garde* thinkers? Wear Chartreuse. If you want to refresh, clarify and stimulate your own creativity, wear Chartreuse. Or, if you just want to be more aware of modern new things wear Chartreuse.

Turquoise

Need a change? Looking to progress? Hunting for a "meaning" for it all? Or, do you just want to attract strong-willed people with diverse interests? Wear Turquoise.

Lavender

Looking to attract someone who is looking for romance and beauty? Someone who will protect you? Wear Lavender. Are you trying to be kinder, more gentle to yourself? Wear Lavender. Looking to prove your refinement to yourself? Wear Lavender. Are you an introvert who needs a tranquillizer to soothe and refine your Spirit? Then Lavender is the color for you!

Indigo

Indigo is worn by someone who wants to intensify Intuitive feelings, to give a Spiritual Meaning to Life, to gain a deeper understanding, gain insight and refine their Intuition.

Salmon

Want to subtly come out of hiding, deal with humanity and confront "things"? Wear Salmon! Want to be more dominant, proud, alert, energetic and enjoy? Wear Salmon.

Olive

Are you looking to attract practical people who have a secure life-style? Wear Olive. Want to find someone to lean on? Or, do you just want to blend in with the crowd? Wear Olive. Need to be more reasonable, rational and positive? Wish to balance your thoughts? Wear Olive.

Magenta

Say you don't want commitment? You'd like a little fantasy, richness and freedom? Wear Magenta. When you need to "loosen up", to "travel" physically, mentally or emotionally--to make fantasy your reality, to dream a little, wear Magenta.

Plum

Wear Plum to feel full, solid, creative, warm and rich. Wear Plum if you are looking to attract a warm and sensitive person. Wear Plum to counter depression and create a feeling of well-being.

Brown

Want to blend in? Relate better physically and materially? To make a statement of "Self"? To aspire to Earthly comforts and riches? To attract substantial people, future employers? To appear dignified, solid and practical? Wear Brown!

Power Neutrals

Gray

Looking to be calmer, more subdued and in control of your emotions? Wear Gray. Need to feel strong, protected, neutral and non-committal? Wear Gray. If you need to quiet down before a big move or power play, appear reserved and dignified, wear Gray.

Black

Black is worn for many reasons. It is worn to protect by repelling. It is worn to be sophisticated, social, to actively search and to seek to attain. It is worn to express emptiness as in a death. It is a neutral that will amplify your feelings whatever they are.

White

White is a neutral that reflects and amplifies your mood. It is worn to feel fresh, to convey freedom, to lighten. It protects by reflection and will amplify your Basic Energy Colorscope--whatever color you are!

Color Accents

Certain color accents can be worn that will not affect your Basic Color Energy. But these colors should be worn only as accents, such as, a belt or sash, shoes or bag, handkerchief or scarf. They must be solid colors, not prints, paislies, plaids or polka dots, and must only be a "splash" of tone. (Note: Colors in parenthesis are not always appropriate. You must "feel" comfortable with these accents or have a specific purpose in mind.)

Blends can wear only the accents that are included in both colors of your blend. For example, Blue/Green could accent with Yellow, Blue, Green, or Indigo omitting Red, Orange and Lavender.

Flashes, use *only* the color of your Basic Personality Profile to gauge your accents. Do not include your Flashes.

Red, you can wear touches of Blue, Yellow, Turquoise or Indigo without affecting your Basic Colorscope.

Yellows can accent with Green, Red, Blue, Indigo, Orange or Chartreuse.

If you are **Blue**, a Red, Yellow, Orange, Green or Indigo is appropriate.

Orange can accent with Red, Yellow, Purple, Green, (Chartreuse), Turquoise or Indigo.

Green you are safe with Yellow, Blue, Lavender and Indigo.

Purple's accents include Magenta, Brown, Red, Green, (Blue), and Orange.

Canteloupe can use a touch of Olive, Purple, (Red) or (Chartreuse).

Beige might choose a Brown, Red, Chartreuse or Salmon.

The selections for **Chartreuse** include, Plum, Blue, Turquoise, Red, Yellow and (Green).

Turquoise can accent with Red, Blue, Beige and Chartreuse.

Lavender remains undisturbed with touches of Purple, Turquoise, Magenta and (Canteloupe).

Indigo can maintain his or her vibration when accenting with Plum, Beige, Magenta or Lavender.

Salmon can take a dash of Magenta, Beige, Brown or Red.

Olive's accents include Brown, Canteloupe, Purple or Red.

Magenta hums along unchanged when accenting with Blue, Red, Salmon or Lavender.

Plum can do with touches of Salmon, Purple, Green, Beige or Lavender.

Brown remains undisturbed with bits of Salmon, Purple, Beige, Red or Orange as accents.

COMFORT COLORS IN THE HOME

Can you remember walking into someone's home for the first time and being ready to move in? Have you visited another and not begin to fathom what the decorator must have been thinking? Been so repulsed by still another it was all you could do to keep from bolting out the door?

A very personal, conscious or unconscious, statement of identity, color also can reflect your mental, emotional and/or physical attitudes, including where you are at, where you would like to be, and what you find stimulating, balancing, or comfort-giving.

So, If you are about to undertake a little redecorating, or are trying to figure out why your neighbor painted his house Chartreuse or a bright Salmon, here are a few hints and a little insight on how color and neutrals comfort in the home.

Red

Red in a home is gay and playful. It can express excitement as comfort, the need for power, or energy.

Yellow

Yellow shoots through a home like a ray of sunshine and helps to clear the air. It reflects someone who has or aspires to positive thought, who is looking for happiness and warmth.

Blue

Blue can be an expression of serenity, introspection, of a need for a "cave". It is a color of "submergence", as in submerged in freedom and a feeling of boundlessness.

Orange

Orange in a home creates a rich, earthy, sensual, open feeling, that combines security with a carefree sense. Many people combine Orange with Yellow to feel light and not too involved.

Beige

Beige in the home is passive and bright, rich and comfortable, elegant and reserved.

Green

Green in a home finds comfort in richness, giving and graciousness. It expresses a seeking for fruitfulness and harmony with nature. When outside work is the all too familiar "rat race", Green puts one back with the "natural order of things".

Purple

Purple shields and protects. In a home it is a show of power. Accents of Purple are creative stimuli and trigger in-depth vision.

Canteloupe

Canteloupe lends fluidity, a sense of freedom and grace to a home. While allowing freedom of thought, it also serves to inspire the dweller to wealth and beauty.

Chartreuse

Soothing and stimulating, clean and warm, Chartreuse engenders a feeling of safety. At once warm and cool, it is comforting and refreshing.

Turquoise

A home with Turquoise is open to new ideas. It expresses transitional comfort and reflects changing values.

Lavender

A home filled with Lavender expresses comfort in romance, idealism and tranquility.

Indigo

A home with Indigo reflects a need for deep spiritual rest.

Salmon

Warmth, life, and sparkle is found in a home with Salmon. The color may be used to make a statement of pride without overstating.

Olive

Olive expresses a need for deep cave-like security.

Magenta

Magenta weaves a fantasy creation, revealing a need for comfort in escape.

Brown

Brown denotes sensuality, a love of "creature comforts". It spells material substance, while reflecting a certain "natural" neutrality.

Plum

Plum in a home symbolizes richness and beauty.

Comfort Neutrals

White

White in a home freshens and lightens. A neutral that simultaneously reflects and dissipates adjacent color accents, white is used when you want to feel free and magnetic, fresh and light. It is a radiant neutral that protects by reflecting incoming energies and amplifying the basic energy of the household and its inhabitants.

Black

Black conveys a sparse coolness, an emptiness, a sensuality. It is an absorptive neutral that picks up the vibration of the adjacent color accents.

Gray

Gray in a home is, at once, neutral, easy and distinguished. This soft neutral also picks up the energy of nearby color accents.

CREATING WITH COLOR IN BRIEF

	To Balance	To Aspire to	To Fine Tune	Comfort in	Reason to Wear	In the Home
Yellow	Sadness	Higher knowledge	The search for conceptual and intellectual understanding	Positive thought	Be noticed/Overtly search Amplify positive thought Feel happy Attract ambitious fun-loving people	Clears the air as "a ray of sunshine" For happiness, warmth, positive thought
Red	Depression Physical Weakness	Power Be dynamic	A clear aggressive statement of Self/Purpose Positively directed physical energy	Power	Show strength Counter physical, emotional, and mental weakness Seek power Become dynamic	Gay and playful Energy accents Power and Excitement as comfort

			Positive thought		Be noticed Counterdepression Show and/or find comfort in power	
Blue	Confusion Restlessness Worry	Spirituality Tranquility Hopeful reaching	Spiritual aspirations Calm	Serenity	Endurance Consistency Peace Aid to Spiritual Aspirations	Serenity, Introspection Submergence in Freedom, boundlessness
Orange	Feeling of Failure Irrationality Lack of Self-Esteem Solitude, loneliness	Sociability Happiness Strength and Security	Pride/ Ambition Energy Practicality Empathy Warm understanding	Comfort	Be more social, outgoing, warm assertive, happy Balance feeling of failure, loneliness Attract individuals/ social groups, leaders/organizers, fun and comfort lovers	Rich Earthy Open Sensual Carefree

	To Balance	To Aspire to	To Fine Tune	Comfort in	Reason to Wear	In the Home
Green	"At oneness" with Earth and Humanity	Peace, Harmony, Unity Subtle Strength through Life of Giving	To the world, "forces of nature" and people around you	Fruitfulness and Giving	Subtle strength To find peace and harmony, unity Attract someone with same mental attitude *(Reasons change with mental attitude and intensity of color)*	Gracious, Giving, Rich In Harmony Seeking to tune in to Nature and the "order of things"
Purple	Creativity and Reality/ Purpose and direction	Strength of Purpose	Creative impulse with creative clarity	Protection	Shield/protection To control others Develop strength of purpose Counter self-fear Stimulate creativity	Show of Power Creative accents In-depth vision Protection

Canteloupe	Lack of Self-Love/ Self-Worth Appreciation of Creativity	Sensitivity/ Gentleness with Strength	Generosity Youthfulness Sensitivity to beauty in all forms	Freedom/ Grace/ Youthfulness Inspiration to wealth and beauty Soft warmth/ hope/giving Thinking freely/feeling alive	To attract youth/ wealth/display beauty To sensitize to be more gentle, but strong To feel youthful, hopeful, giving, worthy To appreciate creativity	Adds fluidity, sense of freedom/ grace Allows free thought Inspires to wealth and beauty
Beige	Emotions Endurance Ability to work on, to be unaffected by a "rival"	Richer, more meaningful life in the physical/ material world	Inner strength Handle oneself without letting "things" get in the way	Self-appreciation Pride Inner strength	To be "neutral"/ conservative/ respectful Balance emotions Attract refinement/ future assets/ bright individuals who make solid physical stand	Rich Elegant comfortable Reserved Passive, but bright

	To Balance	To Aspire to	To Fine Tune	Comfort in	Reason to Wear	In the Home
Chartreuse	Confusion Boredom Inertia	Clear thinking Stimulate creativity Be refreshed	Mental clarity Mental "electricity"/ stimulation	Direction toward the modern, the new-- things that make you feel alive	To feel alive, electric, directed To be more aware of modern new things To attract clear avant garde thinkers To refresh, stimulate, clear creativity	Soothing and stimulating Clean and warm Feeling of safety Comforting and refreshing
Turquoise	Truth seeking	Truth Transition and meaning	Change New ideas thoughts/ perspectives	Mental expansion, an "opening up"	To make a change/progress To find "meaning" in life To attract strong-will people with diverse interests	Transitional comfort Open for new ideas Reflects changing values

Lavender	Spiritual Refinement	Spirituality and idealism	Goodness, spirituality, kindness	Romance Self-kindness Warm, soft, gentle surroundings	Usually to find romance/to attract a protector--someone looking for romance and beauty To be self-kind, gentle/to soothe, tranquillize To prove self-refinement To refine the spirit	Romance Idealism Tranquillity
Indigo	Insight Lack of concentration Mis-interpretation	Intensify feelings, intuition Make life more meaningful	Intuition Understanding of Universal concepts	Deep spiritual rest	To refine intuition To give deep spiritual meaning to life To gain insight	Deep spiritual rest

	To Balance	To Aspire to	To Fine Tune	Comfort in	Reason to Wear	In the Home
Salmon	Dealings with humanity (brings one "out of hiding")	Dominance Energy Enjoyment	Alertness Sensitivity Energy Sociability, Communi-cation skills Power without being overbearing	Security	To be dominant, energetic and enjoy To confront "things" To be proud, alert To subtly come out of hiding!	Shows pride without overstating Gives life, warmth, sparkle
Olive	Unrealistic, negative thought	Be more reasonable, rational	Practical thought Future plans Endurance	Blending in with the crowd Feeling solid and enduring	To be reasonable, rational, positive To blend in To attract someone to lean on/practical, people with secure life-styles	Deep cave-like security

Magenta	"Opening up"--a stepping stone to Spiritual commitment	Hopes and dreams	By lightening surrounding pressures, gives freedom to breathe Frees the spirit	Dreams and Hopes	To have richness, freedom, little or no commitment To make fantasy reality To feel lovely, perfect To dream a little/ To" travel" mentallyand emotionally	Symbol of richness and beauty
Plum	Depression A feeling of well-being	Happy, warm, fulfilling life.	By allowing one to be social while working on the spiritual level	Feeling full, solid, creative, warm, rich	To counter depression Attract a warm sensitive person To feel solid, full, creative, warm and rich	Symbol of richness and beauty

	To Balance	To Aspire to	To Fine Tune	Comfort in	Reason to Wear	In the Home
Brown	Physicality	Earthly comforts	Substantiality	Blending in	To blend in	Denotes sensuality
	Light-headedness	Richness	Material and Physical richness and meaning		To relate better physically and materially	Shows love of creature comforts
	Flightiness	Relate better physically and materially	Endurance		To make a statement of self	Reflects a neutrality, as in nature
					To aspire to earthly wealth and comforts	
					To attract substantial people, future employers	
					To look dignified, solid, practical	

Gray	Emotions (calms, subdues)	Be more distinguished	Strength in neutrality	Reservation Neutrality Protection	For strength Neutrality, non-commitment To hold oneself together, stabilize, subdue emotions Calm before a power play Be distinguished	Neutral (will pick up vibration of color accents) Distinguished Quiet and easy
White	By amplification of your own Basic Energy Pattern	Magnetically, pull, reflect and amplify	One's own Basic Energy	Protection via reflection Attainment via attraction	To feel fresh, light To convey freedom To amplify Self To attain To protect	To freshen, lighten To feel free, magnetic To protect, reflect, amplify Dissipates, while reflecting color accents

	To Balance	To Aspire to	To Fine Tune	Comfort in	Reasons to Wear	In the Home
Black	Change	Actively search, absorb, and amplify	Adventure	Revitalized energy via Strength of Purpose	To protect by repelling To seek to attain To actively search To be social To be sophisticated To express emptiness, as in a death To revitalize To be alluring, seductive	Sensual Sparse Cool, empty A neutral that picks up the character of the color accents

COLOR ACCENTS IN BRIEF

Personality	"Accent"
Beige	Brown Red Chartreuse Salmon
Blue	Red Yellow Orange Green Indigo
Brown	Salmon Purple Beige Red Orange
Canteloupe	Olive Purple (Red) (Chartreuse)
Chartreuse	Plum Blue Turquoise Red Yellow (Green)
Green	Yellow Blue Lavender Indigo
Indigo	Plum Beige Magenta Lavender
Lavender	Purple Turquoise Magenta (Canteloupe)
Magenta	Blue Red Salmon Lavender
Olive	Brown Canteloupe Purple Red
Orange	Red Yellow Purple Green (Chartreuse) Turquoise Indigo
Plum	Salmon Purple Green Beige Lavender
Purple	Magenta Brown Red Green (Blue) Orange

Personality	"Accent"	Personality	"Accent"
Red	Blue Yellow Turquoise Indigo	*Turquoise*	Red Blue Beige Chartreuse
Salmon	Magenta Brown Turquoise Red	*Yellow*	Green Red Blue Indigo Orange Chartreuse

POWER PINK!

Power Pink will not be found in our Personality Profiles--it does not reflect a Basic Energy Pattern. *Power Pink is esoteric. Like white, it carries you above your body to another plateau.*

Power Pink is not a hot pink nor a lipstick pink nor a shocking pink--these equate with Red. The indescribable shade of the most delicate pink that emerges when Red is mixed with so much light that it becomes *nearly white light is Power Pink--a color that exists by way of intent, Power Pink is an intense internal force that transcends to magnetically draw peace, relaxation, youth and love into your Colorscope.*

Although, It may visually clash with some tones, Power Pink can be worn with any color--*it will not alter the vibration of the colors you wear, rather it will enhance, igniting a special light in and around you.*

Unlike the forceful Reds, Oranges or Purples, even when externally worn, the delicate powerful magnetism of Power Pink is an *internal power*. When it is recognized by others, it is because of the magic it is working on and within you.

Different from an aspiring color, such as light Blue, which works externally, *Power Pink is a meditation color that carries you to a special place where you can draw love into your Colorscope, "paint" youth into your face and body, relaxation and peace into your being.*

The particular tone of pink that you will chose is personal. It can be an apricot pink, a salmony pink, an orchid pink, or a combination of pinks that you feel drawn to.

It is a pink that you can focus upon, and breathe into your face, skin and body to grow younger. It is a pink that you can see streaming in rays of light from your heart sending out love into the universe which always returns in kind. It is a pink that you can see settling in around you like a mist to relax and rejuvenate. It is a pink that you can visualize as a whirlwind, yourself in the vortex, as it begins at the base of your feet and moves up and around you in a clockwise direction pulling up, tightening your body, reversing the effects of age and gravity. It is a pink that allows you to transcend your body, taking you out of reality where stress will not affect you.

It is a pink that goes to your soul giving you the license to perform magic!

COLOR ME YOUNG!

As you mediate internally drawing youth through Power Pink, externally you can wrap yourself in Rainbow Colors, painting light and reflecting positive energy into your face and physique. Here's how.

Think of yourself wrapped in *light-filled rainbow ribbons,* the "neon" Magentas, Turquoises, Chartreuses, Oranges, Blues and Yellows that you first notice when you view a rainbow.

***Tune your vibration in this way daily.* Even if you are wearing another color, mentally wrap yourself in rainbow ribbons.**

COLOR ME WEALTHY!

Use your aspiring colors to attract wealth. Blue for your intangible spiritual aspirations, Neutrals, Gray, White and Black, to pick up and amplify your thoughts, emotions and intentions, Beiges to aspire to a more meaningful life in the physical/material world, and Cante-loupes to attract wealth.

You can accent in high key colors to help solidify your intent--just a touch so as not to disturb the vibration you are setting. Orange might be a good accent, since Orange is worn for comfort in "comfort", or Salmon which seeks comfort in security. Brown can also be worn to attract creature comforts. *Check your color charts under "Aspiring", "Comfort" and "Reasons to Wear" colors.*

As you wear your chosen colors, focus on "why" you are wearing the color. It is just as important to feel your intentions as it is to wear and surround yourself with the colors, since neutrals derive their power from the meaning you assign to them.

COLOR ME FAT-FREE!

Nothing, of course, can replace a good diet, lots of water and exercise. But Power Color can certainly help you in your efforts. Here's How.

***When you arise in the morning, drink a glass of water that you have mentally transformed to Red.* This will help to jump-start your metabolism.**

As you eat, keep Forest Green in mind. You might consider deep green glassware or plates or a center-piece or tablecloth.

***When you finish eating, meditate on Cobalt (a deep dark) Blue.* This will slow your digestion.** Have a color swatch in your wallet or a special room in which to relax.

To quell hunger pangs, *drink a glass of mentally transformed Chartreuse water.*

Between meals shrink your intestines, *by mentally wrapping them in Purple.*

SOME INTERESTING READING

Babbitt, Edwin D. The Principles of Light and Color. New Hyde Park, NY: University Books, Inc., 1967.

Birren, Faber. Color Psychology and Color Therapy. New Hyde Park, NY: University Books, Inc., 1961.

Clark, Linda. Ancient Art of Color Therapy. Old Greenwich, CT: The Devin-Adair Co., 1975.

Cousens, Gabriel. Spiritual Nutrition and the Rainbow Diet. Boulder, CO: Cassandra Press, 1986.

Dinshah, Darius. Let There be Light. Malaga, NJ: Dinshah Health Society, 1985.

Hunt, Roland. The Seven Keys to Colour Healing. Essex, England: The C.W. Daniel Co., Ltd., 1971.

Lüscher, Max. The Lüscher Color Test. New York: Washington Square Press, 1969.

Ott, John N. Health and Light. Old Greenwich, CT: The Devin-Adair Co., 1973.

______Light Radiation and You. Greenwich, CT: The Devin-Adair Co., 1982.

______My Ivory Cellar. Chicago: Twentieth Century Press, Inc., 1958.

Ouseley, S.G.J. The Power of the Rays. London: L.N. Fowler & Co. Ltd., 1951.

Wood, Betty. The Healing Power of Color. New York: Destiny Books, 1984.

Steiner, Rudolf. Colour. London: Rudolph Steiner Press, 1982.

all natural holistic resources

for Body ◆ *FACE* ◆ MIND

By Julia Busch

FACELIFT NATURALLY

The At-Home or Anywhere, Painless, Natural Facelift for Men and Women That Really Works!

Using only your hands and *PROVEN TECHNIQUES* as much as 10 years, or more, can be erased easily and naturally in *one month*. The 20 minute face lift, practiced as little as one day a week, involves no oils or creams, expense, scars or convalescence. Author Julia Busch, on cassette, "talks" you through a rejuvenating, relaxing, invigorating ***Facelift***. Included are ***Mini-Lifts*** and ***Tune-up-the-Body Points*** realign and rebalance energy, offering help for sinus, headache, digestion, stress and more... Tension dissolves with the ***Back of the Head and Neck Ritual. Hints for a Fabulous Face*** are included. Your "lift" buttons can be pressed any time, anywhere– in the office, on line at the market, walking the dog, carpooling the kids; in the board-room, bedroom or classroom--and no one will suspect.

Program includes: 2 audio tapes (1:40); removable laminated charts, heavily illustrated Easy to Read Large Type manual in a lock-tight binder.

ISBN 0-9632907-6-2. $59.98.
Book only ISBN 0-9632907-9-7. $14.95.

TREAT YOUR FACE LIKE A SALAD!

Skin Care Naturally, Wrinkle-and-Blemish-Free Recipes and Hints for a Fabu-lishous Face!

The "Julia" of kitchen cosmetics asks, *"So what's in the bowl?"* Then sets out to offer a feast for the face with dress-ings, sauces, marinades and masks for complexions ranging from *Regular Tossed Normal, PotLuck Acne, Fridgeworn Devitalized, Chef's T-Zone Combo, Marinading Mature, Crouton Dry, Olive Oily and Over-Seasoned Sensitive.* The edible-wearables not only save a skillet full of cosmetic cash, but actually revitalize your face with down to earth combos that ladies of the French Court, Cleopatra, great-grandma and some of the leading skin care experts and cosmetic surgeons recommend. Included are: nutrition, special care and regimens for each skin type, aromatherapy and more. Discover *The Freeze Lift, Amazing Skin Firming Masks, Deep Moisturizing "Sun-day Soaks," Sweet Scented Facials, "Seductive Aroma Massage for Two," At-home Alpha Hydroxy Fruity Peels and Deep Cleansers. Softcover.* 256 pages. Illustr. Index. Bibliography.
ISBN 0-9632907-8-9. $14.95.